GW00836592

NICE T

A Collection of New Rugby Writing

Edited by

Stuart Barnes and Mike Seabrook

VICTOR GOLLANCZ

LONDON

First published in Great Britain 1995
by Victor Gollancz
An imprint of the Cassell Group
Wellington House, 125 Strand, London WC2R 0BB

Photoset by Rowland Phototypesetting Ltd,
Bury St Edmunds, Suffolk, and printed in Great Britain by
St Edmundsbury Press Ltd, Bury St Edmunds, Suffolk

Contents

Introduction

MIKE SEABROOK

If ever there was a game of contradictions and paradoxes, it is rugby union. More than any other game, it is the product of that most English of institutions, the boys' public school, yet it is to be found in more countries across the globe than almost any other game, East and West, northern hemisphere and southern, from Romania to Fiji and Samoa, Canada to Japan. It is played with equal enthusiasm and passion by peoples of every human condition and temperament, from Italians to Australians.

Many years ago, British public schools and universities were divided between 'hearties' and 'aesthetes'. The two factions were permanently at war: the hearties despised the aesthetes as simpering effeminates 'of the Oscar Wilde kind', and the aesthetes poured aristocratic scorn on the hearties as the embodiment of philistinism-on-principle. The very concept of 'rugger buggers' epitomized the last word in heartiness; yet by long tradition rugby supporters have been a by-word for civilized and temperate behaviour: well-bred, well-spoken gentlemen, who would not dream of fighting, smashing up garden fences or looting off-licences on their way to the ground.

Most paradoxical of all, perhaps, in the mid-1990s, is that rugby is in many ways both an anachronism whose time has come and a private ritual become a highly profitable public show. Until 1995 it laboured under a jealously – some would say fanatically – guarded tradition of amateurism, complicated laws, invisibility to the spectator – in what is the age of the spectator rather than the player –

of much of what goes on and, most of all, perhaps, the fact that of all games it is the most predictable. Where much of the appeal of many other games is the possibility that a minor team may pull off a feat of giant-killing, rugby is the game in which this is least likely to happen. Yet despite all these apparently powerful reasons why it is not really a game for the last years of the twentieth century, rugby union has claims to be *the* game of the 1990s. While many other games have fallen into varying degrees of disrepute and gradual decline, rugby has become fashionable. It is chic, glamorous; it is a game that is, undoubtedly, on the up.

The ancient maxim that association football is a gentleman's game played by hooligans while rugby is a hooligan's game played by gentlemen contains more truth than many clichés; and in general rugby has avoided the more violent controversies of the post-war years that have bedevilled other games. Association football, for instance, has certainly done much to justify its half of that old adage, with all manner of scandals involving match-rigging, drug abuse, criminal assault, drunken, disorderly and variously corrupt behaviour on the part of players and every known brand of anti-social behaviour from its spectators. Cricket has slipped from its pedestal as a synonym for fair play, self-imposed but rigorous sportsmanship and the gentlemanly spirit, to be rent in public over a variety of murky behaviour. Tennis has been the unfortunate victim of carnivorous professional agents. Athletics has torn itself apart from within over money, its readiness to allow itself to be hijacked in the interests of nationalist politics, and drug-taking in the interests of winning.

Rugby, however, has remained in the public's affection and esteem. Its supporters have retained an image of adult maturity and good cheer that could hardly have stood the game in better stead when set beside the behaviour of soccer spectators. The image of the rugby fan has consistently been rather like that of a character in a 1950s British movie, in which he would be played by Kenneth More, with a cast of supporting characters around him on the terraces at Twickers played by Richard Todd, Dennis Price and Nigel

Stock, with an obligatory parson played by Ian Carmichael. He is well spoken, well educated, very slightly raffish – a wearer of sports jackets and flat caps and even possibly a silk cravat – but certainly a gentleman.

Of course this generalization contains more of caricature than of reality yet it cannot be denied that there has traditionally been very little crowd trouble at rugby matches, although Twickenham and the Arms Park now hold more people than almost any soccer ground in Britain and Murrayfield holds more than any. The conduct of the players on the field has consistently set an incomparably better example to their youthful followers than that of soccer players.

As rugby began to face a few of the problems that have plagued other games on the field, ominous rumblings boded trouble off the field as well. As this book was being prepared, rugby was undergoing one of a seemingly unending series of internal seismic shocks over the vexed question of whether or not it should abandon its hitherto inviolable amateur principles. To some, this seemed like the suicidal abandonment by the beloved game of the one thing that made it what it was, an act of wanton self-mutilation. To others the apparatus of amateurism was a pious fiction, an absurd anachronism kept in place solely by sentimental old men out of touch with the realities of life in the 1990s. And every intermediate shade of opinion was on display between these two irreconcilable extremes.

With this all going on it was inevitable that the image of the game would become equally divided, and so it did – around the personalities of the leading players on the one hand, and the governing body of the game on the other. The players were, unequivocally and emphatically, of their time: glamorous young men in *haute couture* rugby shirts, available to advertise new after-shaves. The traditionalists were led by the committee of the RFU itself. These were seen by their more extreme supporters rather as the *Daily Express* used to portray the police, as the thin blue line between us and anarchy, standing alone between civilization as we knew it and ruin; they were lonely visionaries, embattled in defence of their dream. To the radicals, they were fogbound reactionaries, inhabiting a Utopian fantasy and looking at reality through the wrong end of a telescope.

However, the overwhelming majority of the game's aficionados showed a marked unwillingness to get worked up about it, but carried on playing, watching and enjoying the game in the same quiet way as before. This was rugby people at their best: marked out by calm, a sense of proportion and a strong disinclination to be swept along by hysteria, mass movements or propaganda.

This strain of quiet good sense shows in that the same crowds still turn up to watch when their side is struggling: Welsh rugby has been in a depressed condition in recent years, but there has been no appreciable difference in the spirit at the Arms Park during that difficult time. The same heavily raincoated and wellington-booted crowds turn out every Saturday or Sunday around minor club grounds to get soaked to the skin and chilled to the marrow, and still take enormous pleasure in watching their teams of local men battling away in a mudbath. Their pleasure is, if anything, quickened rather than diminished by the primitiveness of the facilities; and they still perform mighty feats in their own form of scrum-down to get to the bar in the clubhouse afterwards.

As this book goes to press the home countries will be preparing to do battle again for the Five Nations, wondering if England can score yet a fourth Grand Slam, and everywhere else, over a rapidly increasing portion of the globe, club rugby players will be settling into their new season, all of them full of the perennial optimism. And not long after that it will be history. A few will be looking back over their season with their optimism triumphantly justified and rewarded; for most it will have been simply business as usual. The one thing that is certain is that (with the sad exception, whom we should never forget, of the few who have been seriously hurt) they will all have enjoyed themselves; and mercifully, in rugby that's still the main thing, after all.

Made in Hong Kong

SIMON BARNES

The World Cup and I have something in common. We were both made in Hong Kong.

Hong Kong changes for ever all persons and things it touches. Rugby union, for example. The world's dowdiest sport needed only to touch Hong Kong to become transformed. In Hong Kong, rugby union became exotic. Even fantastic. Only Hong Kong, a maverick genius of a place, could have done this.

Rugby is the sport of the clubbable man, and clubs are defined by the people they exclude. But rugby had only to go to Hong Kong to jettison all this nonsense: to become a teeming polyglot polychrome hurly-burly of brotherhood, rivalry and perfect incomprehension.

But more about me. I say I was made in Hong Kong; truer to say re-made. I arrived there in 1978 to work as a down-table sub on the *South China Morning Post*. That was the last year in which I had a proper job. The paper and I parted by mutual consent. That is to say, the editor hated me, and so did his deputy. So I was sacked. Horror, misery, despair: well, I won't go into that now. I might have gone home, or at least, back to England, but the spirit of Hong Kong had already begun to infect me.

A few months later, then. Typewriter getting up a head of steam, getting off the latest piece of work for my growing freelance practice. Business, travel, you name it, I'll write it, from my flat on top of a hill, looking down over the village of Yung Shue Wan, on Lamma island, a short ferry ride from town. Fine place, but that, too, is another story.

The phone rang, and it was the editor of *Outdoors* magazine, a publication long gone, alas. I wonder how many magazines, local, South-East Asian, Pan-Asian, Pacific, global, come out of Hong Kong? And how long each lasts? There always seemed to be more: ten springing up for every one that fell. Hong Kong is that kind of place: land of perfect, insane optimism. A commission, the editor had for me, the stuff of life. So many words (1,500? 2,000? Impossible to remember) at so much a word (did I get him above 50 cents? I fancy not, for I was young and eager to please in those days) and on such and such a subject. Great, but what *are* the Hong Kong Sevens?

So I was told: it was wonderful, all wonderful, and most wonderful of all was Fiji. You haven't seen sport until you've seen Fiji play sevens.

I had friends in town that weekend, so we all went to the cramped little stadium in Happy Valley, the Hong Kong Football Club. The friends paid their entrance, walked in: that dates the occasion all right. We sat there for two days and watched seven-a-side rugby and, yes, it was wonderful enough. Pissed, of course. It is *possible* to watch the Sevens sober, and to enjoy the day or days, and I have proved that on a number of occasions since. An odd sensation it is, too, to be in a stadium of 20,000 people and to be virtually the only sober person there. But I was one of the crowd then, keeping clear of the press box, didn't need to file copy till the middle of next week, so there was nothing to do with the occasion but revel in it, and scribble notes, at first shrewd and coherent, later brilliant, inspired, illegible.

Team of the tournament? Not a doubt about it. And no, not Fiji at all. The *Outdoors* editor had summed up Fiji: 'All tall as coconut trees, all leap like stags, all run like greyhounds.' An imposing bunch, each one capable of picking a rugby ball from the ground with a single hand. The warm-up was a treat: one-handed passes, behind-the-back passes, no-look passes. And playing, of course, with one of those rugby balls that doesn't touch the ground: that sticks firmly to any Fijian hand. Most rugby balls are like that, I was to learn. But the team of the tournament was South Korea. The stage was set for an Australia–Fiji final, and Fiji prepared to stroll through the first appointment of the day, a routine demolition of Korea.

Now rugby union has a great fault: upsets are rare. In all sports, God is on the side of the big battalions, but in rugby union, God hardly ever gives the underdog a chance. A major win against the odds at rugby union is a rare thing indeed. This is an inexorable law of the game, but for sevens, it is suspended. Seven minutes each way: make an early mistake and you're in trouble. In sevens, a mistake is punished by a try: almost invariably. One moment of anxiety, and you find that you have surrendered the field to the opposition. Miss a tackle, drop a pass, and some fleet-footed bastard is disappearing into the distance, scuttling like a rat beneath the posts. With sevens, a game can be won against technically and physically superior opposition.

In fifteens, the might of the pack is all. Eight men silence their individual natures to become a single animal, sixteen legs to shove, sixteen arms to throttle and bind. Big battalions. But in sevens, as in soccer, games can be won regularly against the odds. Certainties have been set aside, and games are won in the collective dementia of team spirit, or in a sudden explosion of individual brilliance. That is the secret of seven-a-side rugby. It also happens to be one of the greatest delights in all sport.

The day belonged not to the individual brilliance of any Fijian, but to the Korean collective dementia. More than most games, rugby finds a comfortable niche in a martial tradition. Korean culture is full of tales of courage, discipline and war. Those fourteen minutes of action brought us an exhibition of the Korean martial tradition: ferociously crew-cut men flinging themselves with mad savagery at the ankles of the Fijians. Fiji enjoyed a height advantage, it seemed, of several feet, but Korea possessed a heart and spirit advantage that was beyond measurement.

Though, in the end, it was measured. The score was 10–6. And, of course, the Koreans went out in the next round, having thoroughly overreached themselves. They were beaten by Western Samoa, who were themselves beaten out of sight by Australia in a lop-sided final. So, in a sense, the tournament was totally buggered up by the Koreans: buggered by courage and self-belief.

That, then, was the secret of the Hong Kong Sevens: a delight in the perfectly improbable. And exotic. I had always believed that France was the only exoticism in world rugby. Otherwise international rugby was the private business of the home nations, plus a few of the old white dominions. A game that suffered from limitations of culture, narrowness of vision, and no understanding at all of the wide world beyond.

Hong Kong does not suffer from these failings. It cannot afford to. The place has reinvented itself time and again. It is the world's least parochial place. It defines itself by its relations with the rest of the world. To do business in Hong Kong is to do business in Taipei, Singapore, Kuala Lumpur, Bangkok, Manila and elsewhere: the United States, Australia, Japan. In Hong Kong, the only outlook possible is international. For a start, the place isn't even self-sufficient in water, let alone food. Soon it will have to import air. The foreign, the exotic, the risky, the bold, the adventurous: this is the way of life. And so rugby union came to Hong Kong to be transformed.

By the time I was covering the Sevens again, I counted myself a Hong Konger through and through. And yes, filing copy from Taipei, Kuala Lumpur, United States, etc. etc. Fiji won the following year, and showed me at last what the *Outdoors* editor had been on about. It rained and everybody had to play with a wet ball. Except Fiji. For them, the ball was magically dry.

My memories of 1981 are clearer. Or perhaps just soberer. There is no escaping the fact that this is a festival of drinking. Hong Kong, by which I mean *gweilo* Hong Kong, or the Hong Kong of the non-Chinese, is a desperately boozy place in that the drinking at times really does have an edge of desperation, if not outright despair. The Sevens seems to carry with it an air of ritual licence, as if all responsibilities can be set aside for one weekend. It is a weekend asking – demanding – to be lost. It is as if the weekend of the Sevens 'doesn't count' in terms of career drinking – like the couple of quick ones in the morning that nobody knows about. And it is the fact that the Monday after the Sevens is always the busiest day of the year for Alcoholics Anonymous. Who won, for Christ's sake? I was there, wasn't I? I cheered. Jesus. Perhaps it really *has* started to get out of hand.

That air of desperation is a genuine part of all Hong Kong life. Hong Kong lives on the edge, has always done so. Hong Kong is not safe. For every story of extraordinary success, there is another of disaster and self-delusion. But back to the sport, and to 1981. The Barbarians sent out a squad this time, led and dominated by a hairy young giant named Andy Ripley. The man was made to play sevens. He should never have wasted his time with that boring fifteen-man stuff. Power and speed: tackling Ripley in that tournament was like tackling a Harley-Davidson. But the most vivid moment came with the most unprepossessing man in Hong Kong that day. A smallish chap – well, everyone looks smallish when he stands next to Ripley – with a baldish head, against Australia in the final. Ball came to Les Cusworth. He hesitated fatally, indecision writ large upon him.

An instant later he was through. His indecision had caused the Australian cover to become for an instant flat-footed. Cusworth, a player capable of brilliant perceptions, saw that and exploited it in a blinding second of opportunism. Speed, yes. You can't do it without speed, but also you need speed of thought. As Pelé said, breaking into verse for the occasion:

> I run much faster
> than those who run
> without thinking.

On a recent visit to Hong Kong, I sat aboard the ferry (I was on my way to visit old friends who still lived on lovely Lamma island) and counted the number of new buildings between Star Ferry and the Macau ferry that had gone up since my first arrival in Hong Kong. There were twenty-three: bloody great towers, fifty and sixty storeys high, shining with reflective glass, vast with optimism and pretension. The Bank of China even has something like rugby posts on its summit: the story goes that they were an afterthought, intended to raise the top a little so that it could count as the tallest building in Hong Kong. Change is part of life everywhere, but in Hong Kong the pace of change is crazy, demonic, possessed.

So it was with the Hong Kong Sevens. The football club was a wonderful venue for the event: cosy and intimate and bringing every spectator virtually on to the pitch. But as the event grew in loveliness and wonder, so more and more people wanted to watch it and couldn't get in. The event was too big for its boots.

It moved a few hundred yards and changed for ever – but not really for the worse. In 1982, it went to the Hong Kong Government Stadium: open, spacious, a track round the pitch. It wouldn't be the same, diehards said, and it wasn't, but then nothing ever is, especially not in Hong Kong.

The organizers of the event also showed a certain too-big-for-their-boots quality when it came to New Zealand. Or if you prefer, a coming-of-age. They threw New Zealand out. The New Zealanders had been in the habit of sending a club team to the event, a reward to the club in question – Here, fellers, you go and have a free trip to Hong Kong, do some shopping, a bit of rugby and a lot of beers, you've earned it, boys.

The Hong Kong Sevens decided it was bigger than that. This was not a weekend jolly in a backward little outpost: this was top-level international sport. And if you want to play, play properly. Send a team of All Blacks. In 1982, the Hong Kong Sevens did not extend an invitation to New Zealand. It was another change.

The Barbarians sent out a team to defend the cup, but went out in the semis to the Scottish Borderers. Fiji were beaten by Australia in a belter of a game in the other semi. I remember throwing a half-filled plastic cup of beer into the air when Fiji scored, but it did no good. My heart, Hong Konger that I was, said Forever Fiji, but it was not to be that year. But the final was a wonderful game, the score 18–14, and the tournament was a triumph for Glen and Mark Ella. The Aboriginal brothers added fantasy to the day. Every year, magic comes from somewhere or someone: if not from Fiji, from crew-cut Koreans, a bald Englishman or flying Aboriginals.

I went to the Sevens next in 1984. It was, without doubt, one of the greatest days of sport I have ever seen. Easily the best day of rugby union. Fit to be mentioned with Linford Christie's Olympic gold, Joe Montana's drive at the Super Bowl, Kent Hrbek's Grand Slam homer at the World Series, Roberto Baggio's goal at the Stadio Olimpico, David Gower in his pomp in the Ashes series of '85. This was sport of the highest calibre.

I was making a return to Hong Kong, flown out as a guest of Cathay Pacific, the airline which, with the Hongkong Bank, is the long-time sponsor of the event. I was to cover the event for *The Times*. First delight was, tee-hee, the elimination of Australia. They drew 10–10, in a classic sevens upset result, against Canada. Who goes into the cup competition, who to the loser's plate? In the end, it was decided on the toss of a coin, and Canada called right.

Fiji. Glorious Fiji. They got into their stride with victories over Western Samoa and the Public School Wanderers (who included in their number a more elderly Andy Ripley, who had never been to a public school).

New Zealand had taken to sevens like a tank to water. They brought to the game ruthlessness of tactics and of tackling. They brought their most uncompromising qualities to the flighty art of sevens – and unlovely it was, too, but impressive, all right. They beat the French Barbarians, then the Irish Wolfhounds. Come the final.

Before it could begin, a bunch of drunken Kiwi spectators ran on to the pitch, leaving their shirts behind them. They performed a *haka*. Very badly. The Fijians watched. Folded arms; faces of stone. A pause followed; the match was about to begin. And then, as one man, the Fijians went down into a crouch. Seven Fijians performed a war-dance of their own: a performance of tingling intensity before a hushed crowd. The All Blacks were out-*haka*-ed, outpsyched – and then outplayed. Lord, what a game it was. But this All Black seven was really good. They got to the final on pure uncompromising merit.

And they got stuffed. They got beaten 26–0 by the greatest display of ball-handling that rugby union has ever seen. Ian Duncan, Fiji's manager, whispered afterwards: 'I've never seen rugby like it.' I would have believed it possible to do such things with a rugby ball and I would have believed it was possible to run that fast. But to do the two things together: now that, surely, was impossible. But no. It happened. I saw it. Sheer bloody magic.

Hong Kong cheered itself hoarse. The Australians had got booed, of course. They always do: pantomime villains. Some even remember how it started: a bit of dirty play against Fiji in the very first tournament, back in 1976. And Fiji, maverick genius: that is the team with which Hong Kong identifies. Certainly not the Hong Kong team. The local team naturally gets a few cheers, yes. They are a little parochial bonus of a day of rampant internationalism. But the closed Hong Kong rugby world – as opposed to the weekend of the Sevens – seems to sum up all the ex-pat stick-in-the-mud qualities that make up the reverse side of Hong Kong's essential craziness.

Hong Kong is full of ambiguities and so is the Festival of the Sevens. Hong Kong is geographically part of China; in 1997, it will return to Chinese government. The Sevens, one of the world's great sporting festivals, is held on Chinese soil, but where are the Chinese? Well, you can find them. Selling beer to *gweilo* drunks, mostly, and sometimes in the audience, always stunningly pretty and on the arms of *gweilo* drunks. But there are no young fellows playing rugby, no gangs of lads sitting in the stands and watching. You don't hear much Cantonese spoken at the Sevens. The sport of the Hong Kong Chinese is soccer. I know. I used to play it with them twice a week, as goalkeeper to my team.

I do not want to be sentimental about Hong Kong, or about the Sevens. A place, an event I love, whose bold, exotic spirit seldom fails to lift the heart. But joys are set about with complications: nothing about Hong Kong is straightforward. You can see simplicity if you want to, but only by closing your eyes to awkward facts.

In 1987, rugby union invented something called the World Cup. A mere fifty years after soccer had invented *the* World Cup, rugby realized that it, too, was a world game. This came as news to a lot of people: but not to anyone who had been to the Hong Kong Sevens. It seemed clear as day that the idea was pinched wholesale from Hong Kong. There they were, the rugby-playing nations of the world: Argentina, the United States, Italy, and, of course, Fiji. The top sides of the world come from just six nations: Britain, Ireland, France, South Africa, Australia and New Zealand. But with the World Cup came a Hong Kong-like destruction of barriers and boundaries.

The greatest treat of all was Western Samoa. It is one of the greatest regrets of my life that I missed their defeat of Wales. But I saw them play the most wonderful thudding, shuddering match against Australia in Pontypool, in soft Welsh rain in that lovely ground carved from a hillside. They reached the quarter-finals, too, finally stopped by Scotland. They had broken, or at least bent, the monopoly of the Big Six.

There is a tendency for rugby to live in the past. It is one of the sports of empire, after all, and tied about with delusions of importance and amateurism. The sport had an unholy relationship with apartheid, which reveals a piercing sense of commitment to the past; a blind eye to the future.

England took part in the World Cup, of course. But they did not send a team to the Hong Kong Sevens until 1995. Only twenty years too late. In the meantime, the Hong Kong Sevens have probably done more to raise the standard of the world's minor rugby nations than any other single factor. The glory of international exposure: what greater gift can be given?

I last went to the Sevens in 1993. It was a weekend made memorable by the individual genius of Waisale Serevi, the Fijian stand-off.

Their demolition of Australia in the semis was something to gladden the heart, and the event was, as ever, a glorious international occasion. Of the four semi-finalists, only Australia had a majority of white faces. Most of the New Zealand squad were of Pacific races.

The New Zealanders were beaten in their own semi, which meant that Western Samoa faced Fiji in the final. And the Hong Kong crowd changed station, abandoned beloved Fiji, and cheered for the newest underdog. Fiji lost a little shape and discipline against their South Pacific rivals, and the Samoans squeaked it, 14–12. A magnificent game. There have been so many.

The Hong Kong Sevens remains a uniquely satisfying event. Something to do with the location, I think. Sport is an expression of optimism: Hong Kong is the most spectacular embodiment of optimism the world has ever seen. I wonder if genius, too, is an aspect of optimism: a self-belief so strong that physical realities fade and disappear in its face. Hong Kong itself is a kind of genius. And it has lent a fragment of itself to the sport of rugby union.

Rugby in Extremis

STEPHEN JONES

How is it possible to love Romania, and especially to love Romanian rugby? Ireland thrashed Romania by 60–0 at Lansdowne Road, Dublin, in the autumn of 1986. This was not a great Irish team but they reduced Romania to a rabble. When Dean, the Irish fly-half, scored the last of the ten Irish tries I looked around. Where on earth was Doja, the Romanian flanker who was supposed to be marking Dean? Back at half-way, I saw him, on one knee, tying his shoelace. He did not care. His morale, his spirit, had gone. When you wear the jersey of your country you are supposed to expand in demeanour, to fill it. Doja's kit seemed several sizes too big. The only player who did seem to play with passion was a young forward, Hari Dumitras.

Ever since the first Romania match I reported, and ever since the first of many visits to Bucharest, it has always been that sullenness that struck me. In the late 1980s it was a sullen country, people walked hunched, there was no gaiety; even the lurid flashes of a neon jungle would have come as a blessed relief among the browns and the greys. Sure, you could appreciate under the decay that they call Bucharest the Paris of Eastern Europe; at its hidden heart and soul, it is a superb city. But even in the big hotels, the food was appalling: at breakfast on the buffet trays lay shrivelled, blackened shapes, which might at one time have been some sort of fruit; chunks of almost pure white fat with a thin stippling of brown indicated some kind of bizarre attempt at bacon. If this is what they have in the big hotels, we said, what are they eating out in the city and in the hinterlands?

21

The city itself reeked with fumes from heavily leaded petrol and ancient exhausts. It was oppressive in other ways too. Later we all found out that the widely received wisdom that one in every four people in the country was an informer for the Securitate was a lie put about by the Securitate. It was a brilliant ploy. It saved that body the problem of recruiting and kept everyone in line with the fiction that anyone they were talking to might report back subversion, or even a joke at the expense of the dictator, Nicolai Ceaucescu.

How could the country's sportsmen not reflect that sullenness? How could the rugby team be expected to play with verve and invention if in modern-day Romania there was nothing in life to inspire? I have seen so many games when Romania simply went out to fulfil a fixture, played a dour style and visibly lost heart when the game began to slip. England thrashed them with minimal resistance when the red rose was seen for the first time on a Romanian field. It was on a hot Bucharest day in 1989 and in the airless stadium it was Romania who were roasted.

I think it was on that Dublin day in 1986 when I first began to love Romania, and its rugby. Admittedly, it was at first a worthless affection drawn from pity. The grim adventures of the Romanian team that Dublin weekend were a story all to themselves. Romanian rugby actually has a long and proud tradition but had become impoverished, first, because the country was impoverished – Ceaucescu sold abroad the produce of an essentially fertile country for foreign currency, fiddled away millions for his vanity and on monstrous schemes to restore a kind of agricultural feudal system – and second, as rugby was not an Olympic sport, what sports funding there was went towards the gymnasts and those others who could almost guarantee glory in the eyes of the outside world.

But it had all become a farce. The Romanian team left Bucharest on a nightmarish journey, in an ancient turboprop plane of TAROM, the national airline, for whom the word chaotic never really seemed to sum up their operation properly. The flight took hours and hours, landed frequently to refuel in various points of

Europe; there were even rumours that no one on board had any means to pay and the fuel had to be, as it were, put on the slate. For that whole journey there was no food on board, not so much as a bread roll.

The team arrived in Dublin late on Friday, tired, hungry and too late to train in any meaningful way. The TAROM crew then went off to secure their accommodation. They had been given an allowance of £2 per night. The city's main hotel was charging £120. The Dublin people rallied round; they were looked after. There were waggish observations in the evening papers that Dublin men had rallied round to offer accommodation to the stewardesses. The team duly, abjectly subsided and they all set off home on their turboprop to a country where next to no one cared, and those who did, now cared less.

The pity was heightened by fury. The leading home countries had always had a reciprocal agreement with the Romanians. They would pay for Romania when Romania visited, getting around the chronic shortage of foreign currency by paying for hotels and transfers and, given that Romania had drawn crowds of between 18,000 and 45,000 in the British Isles for Test matches in the last fifteen years, it was hardly a costly exercise because the gate receipts covered costs at least twenty times over and left a handy profit for the unions, already rich. As the other part of the deal, Romania would pay for incoming teams – it was the only way to proceed because at least then Romania could scrape up a few resources: friends of Romanian rugby would donate some wine for the dinner, they would pool their meat to give enough for the visiting team, hotels were cheaper and could be discounted through government departments. For the post-match dinners, even in the most austere years, the hosts would always put together a colourful event and, by their standards, a lavish spread.

The Irish Rugby Union tore up that agreement, so the Romanians had to pay for themselves in 1986. Hence the turboprop, the starving, the £2 a night when they needed £120. The Scottish Rugby Union also ended the reciprocal agreement. They did so because they were miffed at the poor facilities in Romania and wanted their team to have the best. I recall the Scots visiting Romania in the 1980s, whining about the hotels, whining about a spread of food which, if not a banquet by their standards, was a feast drawn together only after massive sacrifice on the part of their hosts. The Scots whined at the training facilities. Their committee complained at the lack of what from other nations, committee to committee, is usually a regal welcome, full of bonhomie, fine wines and feasting. Because the reciprocal agreement had been torn up, the next time Romania visited Scotland, paying their own way, their travel agent had to beg for money from firms who traded with Romania, and the party had to leave Edinburgh for Heathrow at midnight on the evening of the game. After the post-match dinner had broken up, they boarded buses and set off in the Scotland night. Little wonder that Raducanu, their lock, defected that night. Other squad members disappeared on overseas trips, to resurface in France.

To me, this dreadful denial by the Irish and Scots offended grievously all that rugby was supposed to stand for. To pamper their sleek, well-fed athletic rugby squads, to seal them hermetically from the experience of touring, while denying any help whatsoever to an opposition that was deprived, hungry and had its basic rugby abilities submerged, was a thundering disgrace and unforgivable. I had seen enough to know that Romania at heart are a strong rugby nation; if they were given the same preparation, diet and back-up as one of the Five Nations teams they would hold their own in the Five Nations without any question. They had thrashed Wales in Bucharest in 1984, had always shown a basic strength in their game. I have always felt, too, that Romania is a majestic country where the government, and the fates, simply conspired and got it all horribly wrong. It is not as if the place is a desert, infertile in crop and culture. To see hardship and struggle is one thing, but when it could all have been different, then it is ever more difficult to accept.

I can also remember the effect of a single photograph. When the World Cup came to London in 1991, the teams were entertained at a banquet to launch the event. All sixteen competing teams were there, all in their smartest blazers and flannels. There were two teams to a table, and they sat facing each other. The picture shows the Scots on one side, blazers off, ties askew, laughing and joking, raising glasses towards the camera, blissfully relaxed. And facing them, with almost military bearing, blank-faced, ties held tight, uncomfortably glaring at the camera, are the Romanians. You felt that, deep down, they must be lighter of mood than that; you almost begged them to relax, to have faith in themselves and their rugby, to join in the community. Rugby is a game to shake off dull care, even at its high level. It was a picture to make the heart of a rugby universalist bleed.

The rugby men in Romania were and are as fine as any. I had become acquainted with the likes of Florica Murariu, the great old flanker who was still in the team in the 1980s and part of the conscience of the Romanian game for so long. It was Murariu's influence, as flanker and leader, which dragged Romania to their ascendancy in the early 1980s, when they were good enough, especially in Bucharest, to beat any team and when, after years when they had been afterthoughts and B games on the lists of the major unions, they earned full cap status in the eyes of the world, and deserved it.

After his impressive early game in adversity in Dublin, I had met Hari Dumitras, as outgoing a Romanian as you could experience. These people, holding on in defiance of fate, circumstances and Ceaucescu, became heroes.

The Romanian revolution, as it was then called, came at Christmas 1989, a few months after England had toured, experienced the paranoia – and the megalomania. Words can hardly convey the scale of the palace Ceaucescu built for himself, tearing down tradition and history in central Bucharest, tearing down churches to provide a sweeping avenue up to the soaring, grotesque folly.

The revolution seemed, to us following on TV, dangerous and heady; stories of 80,000 people killed in Timisoara galvanized the world's media; there were little sub-plots, in which desperate gangs of Securitate members were taking on the brave young regular army units who were defending the freedoms newly established by the shooting of Ceaucescu and his harridan wife. Only later we found that the number of deaths had been wildly exaggerated, that there had been few street battles; we heard from Romanian intellectuals that the Communists, remustered, were still in charge and that the tracer bullets we saw screaming across Bucharest were a kind of firework display from propped-up guns to convince the outside world and the rank-and-file Romanians that a battle was taking place, signalling some strategic departure.

But if you leave aside this over-cynicism, there was a change. Romania, and especially Bucharest, became less hunched and morose; a little more fruit and a little more ease gradually appeared. Twickenham staged its own spectacular for the country with a Rugby for Romania match, played between leading European players, which showed the concern for the country and which raised thousands, for kit for the rugby youngsters in the country, and yet also for medical help. The most haunting images of the revolution had been those of the impoverished, abandoned orphanages; the images struck a chord which went beyond sport, beyond simple care for sporting people's pastimes.

A few months after the revolution, the Romanian team arrived in Auch, in Gascony, to play their first match since the revolution, against France. It was, at one time, the worst and the greatest match I have ever seen. By now, Hari Dumitras was his country's captain; the demeanour of the team had changed; they seemed to revel a little in their training. Dumitras even beamed at a pre-match press conference.

There were also two notable firsts. Romanian television had always been dire. When it came on air, which was not frequently during the day, it showed only a catalogue of the so-called achievements of Ceaucescu. Most of the population tuned their receivers so that they could have Bulgarian TV. But a Romanian TV commentator came to Auch, and even if the coverage broke down occasionally, the game was shown live on Romanian TV. Incredibly, the Romanians also had travelling supporters. About sixty made it to Auch. They had driven overland from Romania in two old, wheezing buses; they spilled out stiffly and sat in the stand, waving the Romanian flag – no one in Romania had had time to organize a new one so all Romanians celebrating the new freedoms simply cut out the Ceaucescu emblem from the middle of the old one and waved that. They sang old, once-banned folk songs.

The match was of poor quality. The French were unrecognizable, disjointed and poor. The Romanians were not fluent. But to me, it was a glorious hour and a bit. They were heroic. Their forwards played with passion, standing against relentless French driving and attempts to shake them. Hari Dumitras played a staggering match. He was inspirational, ferocious, relentlessly encouraging. Gelu Ignat, his fly-half, kicked Romania into a 12–6 lead, and in the last ten minutes, as France attacked with desperation, Romania showed a morale and a simple, passionate togetherness that would have graced a New Zealand team.

The whistle went. Romania had won, beaten their oldest enemy. On the field and in the stands, Romanians cried, and hugged each other. The crowd had been incensed with France all afternoon; they booed and jeered and shouted for the resignation of Albert Ferrasse, the autocratic old president of the French Fédération, who sat miserably in the stands. But as Dumitras left the field on his way to the tunnel and the dressing rooms, the jeering stopped. The crowd stood and clapped him from the field. Hari lifted his arms as he reached the tunnel, and waved, beaming.

These days in Bucharest, things are easier, though not easy. An odd combination of foreign firms and privateers have arrived, with their input, technology and, in some cases, black market and bully-ing profiteering. But the country is lifted. Romanian rugby has more heart, less resignation.

Facilities are still spartan and the game still impoverished. The numbers who play are not rising. In 1994, they were thrashed at Twickenham, not, this time, because they did not care, but because back at home preparation was still dreadful, facilities bare, state encouragement low. There were rumours of mismanagement and corruption in the sport, and with the country itself beset with privateers it would be surprising if none had reached rugby. It was now more on grounds of technology and technique, rather than simple morale, that the basic excellence of Romanian rugby was being hidden.

But at least we knew, after Auch, that Romanian rugby was inherently good; that circumstances, often brutal, had hidden its strength but that fortune and facilities could yet bring it to the fore. Hari Dumitras, as did other leading players, departed for France and the glamour of French club rugby; Dumitras continued to lead Romania until recently when, feeling tired in his legs and, perhaps, a little sapped by the sheer magnitude of the struggle behind and the struggle ahead, he retired from international rugby. He should be decorated, a princely figure worthy of the great days of great Romanian rugby men.

On the first day of the Romanian revolution, Florica Murariu approached a roadblock in Bucharest manned by nervous conscripts. He was shot dead, one of several well-known Romanian rugby figures to fall in those days. It had been a tragic misunderstanding.

Standing Room Only

TIM HEALD

I first caught the authentic aroma of rugby football fanmanship in the Twickenham car park *circa* 1951. I would have been seven years old at the time and my recollection – imperfect at this distance – is that my father had taken me to see the Combined Services against the All Blacks. One of our fellow spectators was a chap called 'Chips' Heron, a retired major in the Dorset regiment with a distinctive laugh. He lived in Buntingford and was in the booze business. I remember him once turning up at my parents' house with a barrel of rough cider.

In the car park after the match my father and friends were standing round having a snort when Chips spotted a man selling gas balloons. Quick as a flash he got out one of those old-fashioned flame-throwing cigarette lighters and set off in pursuit of the balloon-seller.

This was my introduction to Twickenham. A middle-aged major skipping round the car park popping balloons with his lighter, cackling with mirth and egged on by his friends. All very silly but I'm sure they paid the man for any balloons destroyed and it caused a lot of more or less innocent laughter.

I started playing the game a year or two later and continued to do so for the best part of a decade. I was sometimes allowed to play fly-half in a very bad team. This I quite enjoyed. In my rather good house team at Sherborne I only scraped in as a wing three-quarter in my final year and, joy oh joy, suddenly learned to tackle. For years this skill had eluded me despite hours of running at a sandbag on a wooden gallows, as if doing bayonet drill. Now, suddenly, in 1961, I cracked it. Two of my victims were stretchered off and I still remember my shameful smirk when one of them shuffled down the aisle in next morning's chapel. One leg was in plaster and he was on crutches. 'All my own work,' I said to myself.

Even if you have only played a game at a rudimentary level it does enhance your appreciation of it as a spectator. Thanks to my schooldays, I can begin to understand how difficult the easy-looking things are, how cold it can be in hail, how frightening it can be to be trapped at the bottom of a loose scrum. And so on. Of course, my sense of all this is only rudimentary because I wasn't very good and I retired early. On arriving at Oxford one of the first people I saw was the university blue Freddie Craig, who played in the second row for Ulster. He was huge. I was alarmed by the look of him and hung up my boots immediately.

Because of this my views on the rolling maul, the necessity of crossing the gain-line and all the other jargon-ridden tactics of modern rugby are primitive. In the fifties and sixties the ball was leather and, especially in rain, much heavier; the boots were leather, too, with reinforced toecaps, so the art of place-kicking then – a straight swing with the toe while scrum-half held the ball – was utterly unlike the side-on hoof with the instep. And the rules have kept changing – not always for the better.

Therefore those of us who learned and played rugger in the fifties and sixties don't always have a perfect knowledge of what is now allowable, or of what is tactically sound. But we do, I think, have a sense of the fundamentals. In the same way, someone who fought at Agincourt or even El Alamein would not have understood the technicalities of the Gulf War but he would have recognized the fear, the excitement, the pumping of adrenalin and all the other constants of conflict.

I returned to Twickenham from time to time during my schooldays, always in the company of my father. We usually sat in the West Stand. There were parties in the car park and I came to build up a whole series of Twickenham associations which remain with me to this day, even though the place has changed so dramatically. I remember pipe tobacco, sometimes that distinctive vanilla-ish Balkan sobranie. I remember the laughter and noise of middle-aged men away from their women-folk in that wardroom/officer's-mess fashion. I remember 'British Warm' Army greatcoats, and remonstration with the referee – 'Oh, come on, Cooper.' I remember bitter cold somehow accentuated by those great gaunt olive green stands: they seemed to be constructed of corrugated iron and plywood and when, as sometimes happened, the sitters stamped their feet in unison the whole structure shook like a Los Angeles skyscraper in an earthquake. Above all, I remember the excitement of watching a live match and the thrill you can never really get from second-hand spectatorship on TV and radio.

In those years, however, we always *sat* at Twickenham. My only experience of *standing* to watch rugger was at Sherborne. Watching the 1st XV on a Saturday afternoon was compulsory. School prefects and sixth formers sat on benches while their juniors stood on duckboards behind them. Those games were exciting: open, fast and fair. The players were very fit – much more so than most of the first-class players of the day – and almost every match was a Derby. The main encouragement we offered was the single word 'School', bayed in bass and tenor, sometimes in harmony, sometimes counterpoint. 'School . . . school . . . school!' used to echo up and down the line sounding like the call of rutting stags. Afterwards we would head off to the tuckshop, or 'Toey', for an eightpenny-ha'penny steak and kidney pie and a bottle of Vimto.

It was these occasions that taught me the difference between being a standing and a sitting spectator. Certainly sitting was more restful, even civilized, but it was nowhere near as invigorating. The jostling among the juniors gave you a feeling of participation and when a try was scored or your fly-half made a break you leaped up and down, exulting as much as the players themselves. There was a camaraderie among those who stood which was quite lacking in those who merely sat.

My pleasure in standing was later enhanced by soccer matches.

I used to stand on the terraces to watch an Oxford United team captained by burly Ron Atkinson, and later, when working in London, I accompanied my friend Fred to the Shed at Chelsea in the days of Osgood and Hudson and Charlie Cooke. One day we even ventured east to Millwall, where the atmosphere was over-vigorous and the crowd went mad after Derek Dougan scored a late equalizer for Wolverhampton Wanderers. There was blood and glass and men rocking tube trains back and forth and spitting through the doors.

Perhaps it was the early stirrings of that sort of soccer hooli-ganism which sent me back to Twickenham in the mid and later sixties and which introduced me to the pleasures of the old South Stand which I continued to enjoy, year in, year out, for the best part of twenty years or more.

It is not long gone so most serious followers of the game will remember it. It was not beautiful but it worked. As I remember it was little more than a row of concrete steps dotted with metal stanchions and the occasional solid buttress or bulwark immediately above the staircase entrances. At the top there was not only a fine view of the pitch but also, if the play became tedious, of the terraces across the river at Richmond where Mick Jagger now has a house. In this respect it slightly resembled the riverside stand at Fulham Football Ground. From the top of that you used to be able to look down on the Thames and watch the rowing.

It was Philip Howard of *The Times* who first invited me on to the South Terrace. Not, of course, that you needed an invitation just to get on to the stand but you did need an invitation to join the Howard party. In those days tickets were relatively easy to come by. This was long before Twickenham had become a place of expense-account entertainment and executive boxes, and the Howard party was usually considerable. There was one Calcutta Cup game when there must have been almost thirty of us and we could have staged an England–Scotland match of our own.

Howard himself played for Eton – not, as I frequently remind him, a conspicuous hotbed of the game – for his Oxford college and for one or other of the London Scottish XVs. His father, Peter, the original Cross Bencher of the *Sunday Express* and a famous leading light in Moral Rearmament, captained the England XV before the war. So Howard's pedigree for running the South Terrace onlookers was highly presentable.

An essential adjunct, however, was his wife Myrtle. Myrtle is a Scot and a brilliant cook-caterer in a fine Scottish tradition. Myrtle's picnic hamper, which invariably included liberally sherried consommé, smoked salmon sandwiches and pheasant shot in Ayrshire and hung in the Howards' flat in Ladbroke Grove, was absolutely central to all South Terrace excursions.

On international days Twickenham does not open its gates until midday. There were no reserved places on the terrace but it was very important that our party could camp behind one of the staircases. This gave you a wall to lean against – quite important in the seething scrum which built up shortly before kick-off – and also an unimpeded view of play. Our party nearly always included quite small children. Also one of our stalwarts, Jeanette – now, I understand, the medical officer for Saracens, then a GP in North London – is quite a tiny person and needed a parapet to see over. She was quickly christened 'The Chinese Lady Doctor', which, I suppose, sounds racist and sexist these days but then seemed only affectionate and descriptive.

The drill on match days was that we would all form up at the barred gates some time before noon and then one of the women or children – preferably more than one – would claim to be taken short and would ask if they could make use of the facilities within the ground. Even the most hatchet-faced curmudgeon of a steward fell for this ploy. There were no public lavatories immediately outside the ground and Myrtle, Jeanette and/or the children managed to look so distraught and appealing that they were invariably able to waltz into the ground and take up their position just behind the right-hand upright looking north.

When the gates opened a few minutes later the rest of us would charge in with our hampers, Thermoses, hip-flasks, travelling rugs and other necessary impedimenta and join our advance party for the serious picnic.

Sometimes kick-off was not until three o'clock so that feasting had a good three hours to run. Quaffing often went on throughout the game, particularly in the days before political correctness. (Myrtle, usually the only driver, was virtually teetotal. On at least one occasion several male members of the party literally fell out on to the Notting Hill pavement when Myrtle opened the back door of the Volvo.)

Because of the copious alcohol intake one or two were well away even before the game began. A prime offender in this regard was Myrtle's Uncle Monty, now alas deceased. Uncle Monty always liked a dram and once or twice behaved indecorously as a result. The worst such occasion was a Welsh match. Eventually the RFU had become worried about the overcrowding on the terrace and limited – or seemed to limit – the number of tickets. In the sixties and seventies, however, there was virtually no room for movement. Agile latecomers would sometimes scale our barricade, dangerously, though as far as I can remember no one was ever seriously hurt. Occasionally someone, usually small, would be passed down over the heads of the crowd if they needed to get out.

Conventional progress on foot through the massed bodies was not possible between about half an hour before kick-off until the final whistle. On the day of Uncle Monty's match a number of Welsh supporters, themselves pretty much the worse for wear, arrived late – not an unusual occurrence – and were unable to make further progress because of the press of people. As they stood underneath us Uncle Monty suddenly leaned over the parapet and was violently and uncontrollably sick. His victims below were impotent. They couldn't move forward to get even with their assailant; neither could they move back to perform ablutions because yet more latecomers had piled in behind them. All they could do was stand and shout Celtic obscenities.

This was an ugly moment. A little later in his career Uncle Monty became involved in a dispute involving a policeman's helmet, which was only resolved by the timely intervention of the Howard brothers. As the old boy had poor sight by then, and had trouble seeing to the far end of the ground even before having a drink, it was thought prudent to pension him off. I last heard of him in an old people's home whence emanated fearful stories of his predatory attempts on the female inmates. Despite the occasional excesses I missed Monty, for he was the first of the original regulars to depart.

Considering the crush and the alcohol, we had remarkably little trouble even though the south was where the visiting fans invariably gathered. We were always welcoming to visitors' children and tried to find space for them among our own children and the Chinese Lady Doctor at the front of our informal enclosure. The enemy were, on the whole, well disposed, though it was advisable to wear gumboots for the Welsh match. (I never understood why they offended on this score more than other nationalities.)

Given the Howards' Anglo-Scots background (Philip did National Service with the Black Watch) the Calcutta Cup match was always likely to be a needle occasion but it was mostly good-natured. We minded very much, it seemed to me, being beaten by the Scots and the Welsh, but were none too bothered if beaten by the French and hardly at all when we lost to the Irish. However, the nearest to nastiness, apart from the Uncle Monty incidents, was when an elderly Irish gentleman persisted in beating one of us over the head with his umbrella whenever the Irish did anything of note. Unfortunately he singled out a friend of mine called John Thomson.

Thomson was a lovely, red-faced fat man, an amateur farrier, former military policeman and a *Daily Express* leader writer in the days when they rivalled the pithy nationalism of later *Sun* headlines. He was no lover of the Irish and did not take kindly to being beaten with one of their umbrellas, but he did no more than go even redder in the face than usual and shout a lot. Luckily we won that day so he felt able to be magnanimous.

I enjoyed the French matches as much as any and for a variety of reasons. Their style of play was almost always exhilarating. While we stood in the south moaning the perennial lament of 'Give it to Duckham . . . Give it to Duckham,' they always seemed to have any number of small swarthy men from the Basque country, or thereabouts, all of whom seemed eager to run the ball from everywhere but best of all from inside their own 25.

Their supporters exhibited just as much panache. There were always one or two cockerels released on to the pitch at some point but the best, and for years most consistent, aspect of the French support was a band from Dax. They dressed rather like hospital interns in off-white smocks, had a strong brass section and were much given to carrying outsize loaves of bread on their heads. I never understood the precise significance of this but vaguely assumed it was a Gallic gastronomic taunt, a two-fingered gesture at the English sliced white loaf in plastic wrapper. In retaliation the Howard picnic always surpassed itself at the French match. Marcel brought outsize chocolate and coffee éclairs; my wife (who only came once and loathed it) baked creamy quiche Lorraine; an Anglo-French couple provided tarte Tatin with a proper glaze; and the plonk was upgraded to passable claret.

In contrast, English hoop-la, outside our picnic area, has always seemed anaemic. I suppose the most peculiar moment was when the well-endowed Erika Roe streaked naked across the turf almost immediately in front of us. Streaking seems to be a particularly English pastime and I don't recall any of our Celtic competitors entering a naked runner of either sex. Another time a man stripped to the buff in the depths of winter and climbed on to the roof of the bar behind the West Stand where he remained for a good quarter of an hour. I suppose he had imbibed as freely as Uncle Monty but even so it's a strange way of drawing attention to yourself – and it was very cold, even with an overcoat and scarf.

In similarly exhibitionist, though non-nudist, vein, there was for years the man from Bournemouth who came along dressed in a scarlet tailcoat, grey top hat and Union Jack waistcoat. His name was Bailey and he's dead now. He used to parade round the perimeter before kick-off waving a flag and making Churchillian V signs. We always gave him a wave back and a ribald remark as he passed our position but there was something sad about him. An odd way to pass your spare time. On the other hand, he always got into the ground and he had an enviably close-up view of play.

We nearly always had good bands though never the best of all – now a regular fixture on grand occasions at Lord's – the black-cloaked, yellow-stockinged band of Christ's Hospital in Sussex. The Twickenham bands have usually been conventional military ones and that tradition at least persists. Once, and only once, the RFU imported an American marching band called, I think, 'Marching M'zou' complete with leggy drum majorettes. It was a freezing day with horizontal sleet and, for some reason, the ticket supply had frozen too. The only regulars there were the Chinese Lady Doctor and my father-in-law, who played for Sedbergh and Balliol. It was bad luck to have that band on that day. The Grenadiers would have been protected by bearskins and greatcoats but the girls were strutting their stuff in tights. Unsurprisingly they have never been back.

Music – of a sort – has always been part of rugger and bands have always been part of Twickenham. But the true spectator music has, of course, been choral. At school we had a football song, never sung from the touchline but only by the XV at an end-of-term concert. 'Follow up! Follow up! Collar him! Down him! Well played all!' The Welsh, of course, are past masters, and even on the South Terrace their visiting chorus could manage a passable 'Cwm Rhondda' or 'Sospan Fach'. The French sang the Marseillaise with brio and the Irish, latterly, 'Molly Malone'. The Scots never sang much until they invented a new song, but that never seemed to travel much beyond Murrayfield. The English were always limp with their attempt to follow the band with the National Anthem. Once or twice we tried 'Land of Hope and Glory' and then in the last days of the terrace 'Swing Low, Sweet Chariot' became the red rose hymn. It never worked for me and my most memorable choral moment remains an England–America game when my friend

Barney delivered the whole of the 'Star Spangled Banner' fortissimo and word perfect. The Americans in front could only stand and cheer.

There's no question that the real carnivals were the internationals but there were other, lesser, matches where the South Terrace was a good place to stand. I nearly always eschewed the Middlesex Sevens and the Oxford and Cambridge matches on the – no doubt wrong-headed – grounds that these attracted hardy annuals and not regulars such as ourselves. Alan Watkins, a proper, if contentious, aficionado once described me kindly as *'un homme serieux'* when it came to rugger-watching. I still don't really regard either of these occasions as truly *'serieux'*.

The smaller games I really enjoyed were the early-season ones when Harlequins played the great Welsh clubs and the England trial in January. The latter once, surely, took place on New Year's Day. Certainly I and a handful of standing-only watchers saw an incandescent tyro performance by the about-to-be England full-back Jonathan Webb on a frosty January afternoon. And there were some memorable Anglo-Welsh duels. I remember one between Quins and Swansea when Olver, the Harlequins captain, and Robert Jones, his Swansea opposite number, were both disputing almost all the referee's decisions. The difference was that Olver, always a cheeky chap, seemed to be doing so with humour and a grin whereas Jones was making a surly grudge out of it. The result of this was that Swansea kept getting walked back whereas Harlequins got the rub every time. I was subsequently told that the referee was Olver's brother-in-law.

Part of the joy of these club games was that you could hear everything from the field – the thwack of boot on ball and of shoulder on buttock, the abstruse line-out calls and the general chit-chat, that was obscured by the cacophony of the crowd in the internationals.

Also the mood among those of us standing on the South Terrace was quite different from the frantic sweat and clamour of the packed internationals. At the trial and at the club games there were so few of us that you could stroll about, borrow a programme, and above all exchange gossip.

'Whatever's happened to Hunter's knee?'

'Gareth's a stone overweight.'

'I still say you can't ignore Harriman's pace.'

'He had a dreadful game against Wasps.'

'Fancy a beer?'

And so on.

Many of the hard core of that crew are dead, all gone along with the South Terrace itself. My brother from Somerset, as keen as any, finally rebelled when he was strip-searched by a baboon from the Guards Depot at Windsor and had a plastic bottle of ginger beer and a tub of olives confiscated on the grounds that they could have been used as offensive weapons. 'Full-back pelted by olives!'

Uncle Monty is long dead; so is the rubicund *Express* leader writer John Thomson; so is my father-in-law.

One or two of the children went on to play. Philip Howard's son Jock was fly-half for St Andrew's University; my daughter Emma, once a counterfeit ladies'-loo claimant, won two half blues as the Oxford University women's hooker and was complimented on her play by Clive Norling.

Mostly, however, we have simply faded away under the onslaught of the new cantilevered sitting-only edifice where our old concrete monster used to be. We find it difficult even to get tickets these days, not, for the most part, being directors of Bloggs, Bloggs, Bloggs, Ritzi-Spivvo and Bloggs, or prepared to pay ludicrous sums to the burly tattooed men who lurk outside the gates.

Sad. I have just been reading a memoir of my old school in which the writer remarks that when, during a reading of the *Agamemnon*, an aeroplane flew overhead, the master would cease and say, 'Let us pause awhile as progress passes.' It's how I feel about the new Twickenham and the new South Stand. The saddest aspect, however, is that the pause seems permanent.

We have gone and our time is past. Forget the wicker hampers and the hand-hung pheasant; forget the men from Dax with the bread on their heads; forget chaos and gumboots for the Welsh; forget Uncle Monty; forget the camaraderie of passing people over the heads of that swirling sweaty scrum.

Hello, brave world of bums on seats! Hail, the executive box!

Chips Heron, where art thou now? And, oh, for a balloon to prick.

Et Voilà!

FRANK KEATING

That Carl Lewis of the giraffe world, Andy Ripley, once said that the only satisfactory way to explain the feeling of scoring a try in front of a packed house in an international match was with the immortal words, 'Well, Brian, I somehow found the ball in my hands – and next thing I knew it was in the back of the net.' Quite so. Tries in rugby football, be they mundane bullocky things, close-quarter heave-hos, or convulsively exciting crescendos of operatic grandeur, are invariably instinctive spur-of-the-moment, almost transcendental happenings in which the perpetrators are usually the last to know what took place – the last to 'talk us through it, Brian'.

A veteran alickadoo, a nice old boy with his wits about him, was boasting that he saw the most famous try of the century, scored by one Archibald Leslie Gracie for Scotland against Wales in February 1932. Pull the other one, I said. I'd heard of A. L. Gracie, Scotland's Oxford blue and missionary friend of 'Chariots' Liddell, but I certainly had not heard of his try. I looked it up in the indispensable doorstop *The Complete Who's Who of International Rugby*, which said:

Carried shoulder high by Welsh spectators after scoring a remarkable late try which won the match v. Wales 3.2.23. The ingredients of what was described as one of rugby's greatest tries were an overhead pass, a diagonal scything run, a final dummy pass and a perilous run back inside along the dead-ball line with Welsh defenders in hot pursuit. So close to the dead-ball line

41

was Gracie that when he eventually grounded, one of his boots struck a small boy who lost some teeth.

Mmm, not bad. My old fellow might have had a point. But not as indisputable a one as my late Uncle John, a Cork man, who died in the middle 1950s bequeathing to me the certitude that *he* had witnessed the first 'great try of the century', scored by Basil Maclear (a Dublin Fusilier stationed at Cork's Fermoy) for Ireland against the 1906 Springboks. This remained simple gospel truth in our family. For the purposes of research in the task at present before me, I burrowed into the musty dust of newspaper archive to come up with two on-the-spot scribblers to verify Uncle John's flawless integrity: the grand old 'Dromio' of the *South Wales Argus* and the more-than-objective Edwardian back-page hack E. H. D. Sewell.
Dromio first:

At the beginning of the second half the score was 12–3 in the Springboks' favour. Parke, the lawn tennis player, kicked a penalty goal to make it 12–6; then, in the middle of a sustained South African attack on the Irish line, Maclear intercepted a pass and set out on his long trek towards the enemy line, beginning with a flying leap as he took the ball, and then going straight on. He had very nearly a hundred yards to go but, with a combination of force and swiftness, he passed man after man until he reached the half-way line. As the whole South African side had been up in the attack, there was nobody between him and a try but the full-back, Steven Joubert, and, of course, the second half of the field. The back made to tackle his man and was half bowled over. Maclear went on and the back came after him; there was a second tackle, courageous but only half-successful. For the next few yards Maclear staggered along, carrying the full-back draped around him like a cloak. Then, with a hand-off that was a gesture of royal dismissal, he broke away and scored.

Sitting next to 'Dromio' (I dare say) was Sewell:

Joubert is a small but very plucky back and it needed three hand-offs before Maclear, going a cracker all the time, finally disposed of this terrier, and was able to finish his gallop with a try about midway 'twixt post and corner. Nowhere else at a Rugger ground have I heard such a din as then arose. The mere sight of such a splendid figure of a man as was Maclear going all out on business on a Rugger field is not seen every day. Inasmuch as, added to that, was the fact that he was on an Irish ground in an Irish jersey, and the try might prove to be the turning-point in what was in any event sure to be a very close thing, well, there was ample excuse for the Whirroos and Be Jabers to become unusually vocal! I, at all events, have nowhere else at any game witnessed or heard such a scene.

Four years later, Twickenham was opened, and England appointed Adrian Stoop as captain for the first ever international match to be played at the newly built arena, surrounded by orchards, allotments and nursery gardens, ten miles from the city, just south of the Thames and hard on the River Crane. It was a tremendous occasion, a fiesta. The King was in the Royal Box, and the stadium, not yet splintery and venerable as it was to become, was rafter-packed with celebrants. 'Throughout the morning,' reported the *Illustrated London News*, 'the throng continued to pour into the picturesque country village of Twickenham . . .'

While he had been, so to say, 'sitting on the bench', for two years, Stoop had cemented his ideas about half-back play; and now he had, also back again, the irrepressible Gent, a 'real' scrum-half if ever there was one, working at the back row's heels. The teams were introduced to the King. Then Stoop won the toss. Wales to kick off. Of a sudden, the vast, buzzing multitude are pin-drop silent for a split second as the Scottish referee, John Dewar Dallas, raises his left hand before blowing his whistle . . . Ben Gronow, of Bridgend, kicks off towards the right touchline, deep into England's 25 . . . Stoop catches it calmly . . . He feints to the right as the Welsh thunder down on them . . . He's going left, lancing fast across the midfield . . . He's up almost to his 10-yard line as Wales attempt to regroup . . . They are across at him now . . . He puts up a short kick . . . a beauty . . . Jones goes down on it desperately, but the English are at him like tigers . . . A fierce maul . . . The ball's out for England . . . Gent like an arrow to Stoop . . . Stoop dummies his man and hands on to Solomon at pace . . . The Cornishman's ripped through his man and passes to Birkett . . . Only Jack Bancroft to beat . . . Birkett draws the full-back . . . and flips it to Chapman, his winger . . . Chapman must score . . . *Chapman scores.*

No radio then, of course. But that is how it might have sounded. For it really did happen. Twickenham's first ever try – within a minute of the kick-off and inspired by Adrian Stoop in his first match as captain. Many years later, Stoop recalled it with typical modesty and a spiky dismissal of one of his forwards, Dyne Smith, a stockbroker and forward 'donkey':

I caught the ball from the Welsh kick-off, feinted to the right to pin the Welsh forwards, and then swung left and through them. I put up a short kick when I found myself involved with the Welsh backs; then there was a scramble and the ball went out to Chapman, who scored. D. F. Smith claimed the other day that he was mixed up in it all; but as he is still under the impression that he fielded the kick-off before passing it to me his evidence is worth nothing.

Cornishmen still tell a bitter-sweet story about England's centre that day, their compatriot Bert Solomon, whom they still laud in the Duchy as the grandest of all their grandeur. He played a blinder, but it was the only game he was to play for England. He had come up on the milk train from Redruth to Paddington, then battled his way with the festive crowds jamming the trains from Waterloo to Twickenham, his boots strung round his neck. He made it within minutes of kick-off and introduced himself to Stoop. 'How do you like your passes, old man?' Stoop enquired of his new inside-centre.

Bert replied, in his broad-as-Bodmin accent, 'Juss thraw ball out, boy, an' I'll catch 'um.' Stoop's eyebrow arched. So out they went; and within a minute, of course, Stoop and Solomon had helped conspire and conjure up that superlative opening try.

Just on half-time, Stoop again fed Solomon at speed. As the RFU's centenary history had it, sixty years later: 'Solomon, 40 yards out, sold the Welsh champion, Bancroft, an outrageous dummy before running on, untouched, to score at the Welsh posts.' It settled the match. England won by 11–6, their first victory over Wales since 1898. England went on to win the championship, and Wales were not to win at Twickenham for another twenty-three years.

'I say, old boy,' said the amazed and impressed Stoop when Bert returned to the half-way line after his spectacular run, 'which school did you say you were at?' Bert lied. Instead of the truth, which was Trewirgie Boys' School, he found himself saying, 'Trewirgie *College.*'

That fib made him ashamed. He had no time for these clip-vowelled dilettantes. At the final whistle, he changed quickly, muttered his farewells, battled his way back to Paddington, waited for the milk train home and never once replied to the unending stream of postcards from Twickenham pleading with him to play for England again. He remained in his Redruth butcher's shop, a true hero among his own.

Following that, everyone stopped describing rugby's tries in detail. Perhaps there weren't any worth the purple Quink. Possibly the game changed in a couple of decades interrupted by the obscene carnage of the Great War – and rugby itself became almost a grotesque parody of trench warfare with muddy forward-based slogs for advancement and possession and close-quarter tries, whether scored by anonymous members of the pack or wing-men needing just an eruptive hop-step-and-dive to flop over at the flag. The England XV, for instance, was captained both before and after the 1914–18 war by the lugubriously indomitable maestro and matelot W. J. A. Davies, who organized the attack with a staunch deliberation, by all accounts, but was no fancy-pants in the matter of spectacular tries.

Another household name (well, almost) whose international career bridged each end of that war was the lily-whites' wing-threequarter Cyril Lowe. In the war, Lowe ended as a group captain in the pioneering Royal Flying Corps. He bagged nine German planes – but on the wing for England after the Armistice his scoring was less successful and he was starved of the ball, just as, aeons later, such coruscating touchline tramplers as David Duckham and the young Rory Underwood became. So hungry for a pass was Lowe that when he finally received one at Twickenham in an international it caused such consternation that one in the crowd, P. G. Wodehouse (fellow alumnus of Lowe's at Dulwich), was moved to write a poem on the moment's 'shock, horror' of Lowe being given the ball:

> There he stood, poor little chappie,
> Looking lonely and unhappy,
> > While the other players frolicked with the ball
> For he knew he could not mingle
> In the fun with Coates and Dingle;
> > He could simply go on tackling – that was all.
> I had stopped to light my briar,
> For the wind was getting higher,
> > When a thousand voices screamed a startled 'Oh!'
> I looked up. A try or something?
> Then sat gaping like a dumb thing.
> > My children, somebody has passed to Lowe.

The Springboks from South Africa were invincible between the wars and their game, based on a mighty pack and a relentless punter at fly-half, Bennie Osler, was unimaginatively copied by all their opponents. It made for a fearfully dull game. Odd shafts of sunlight glinted through. For Wales, there was Ronnie Boon's famous try to beat England at Twickenham in 1933, and the legendary score fashioned by Wilf Wooller two years later at the Arms Park, which ensured victory by a point – 13 – 12 – against the All Blacks, and which the grand old man of Welsh sport was still happy to recall well into his eighties as the very century itself was running out of steam:

Wales heeled from a set scrummage on the half-way line towards the South Stand. Haydn Tanner's swift pass was reached, with his fingertips, by Cliff Jones who shot off like a jet. I was at top speed when I got his pass – and Claude Davey was cutting towards me for an inside break when I realized that Oliver, who was marking him, had been drawn in too. I checked, ran round Claude and inside the New Zealand wing Ball and was away in the open towards the Taff end. I sensed a covering wing-forward; All Black full-back Gilbert moved into my path; no sign of my right-wing, Geoffrey Rees-Jones. I tapped the ball over Gilbert's head, not high – 20 feet, maybe – a much-practised short kick. I ran on to the dropping ball with the goal-line a few yards distant. No one in my way, I must score.

The ball hit ground that was hard from overnight frost and rose perpendicularly. I grabbed at it, but it was too high and I missed it, shooting on into the thick straw behind the dead-ball line. It was as I hit it that I heard the crowd roar, hysterically loudly. I did not know what had happened, but as I looked back to the corner I saw Rees-Jones, ball and all, lying over the goal-line. The crowd were in an uproar, the noise deafening. Hats, which were worn in those days, sailed up into the air. Arms were raised. With three minutes to go Wales had scored and won an historic victory.

When I put together the final seconds, I learned that the ball had eluded not only me but also the turning All Black full-back Gilbert. Rees-Jones, coming up behind, had caught it to score wide out.

It all happened four days before Christmas 1935. A fortnight later, on 4 January at Twickenham, England were waiting for the New

Zealanders – England and the son of the former head of the Russian Tsar's Imperial Horse Guards, Prince Alexander Obolensky. England won 13–0, and Ross MacDonald was in the press box:

> Gradually England managed to push the New Zealanders back and there was a scrum in midfield. Behind the scrum the back line stretched out – Gadney, Candler, Cranmer, Gerrard and Obolensky. Obo stood waiting out there on the right wing, a couple of yards inside the England half. England got the ball. From Gadney to Candler to Cranmer. A break and Cranmer was off upfield. But the All Blacks were quick to scuttle back in defence and he was hemmed in. He passed infield to fly-half Candler. Again hemmed in. But Obolensky was there in support on his right. The All Blacks converged on his side of the field, since he was obviously going to try to repeat the 40-yard dash he had done up the touchline earlier to open England's score.
>
> I was sitting in the press box in the East Stand and was virtually behind Obolensky as he got the ball. I could see, as though through his eyes, the situation that confronted him. His opposing wing had been drawn in to counter the Cranmer break, so it was indeed obvious to go up the touchline. But the All Blacks full-back Gilbert, centre Oliver and colleagues were moving over to do their best to block that avenue.
>
> I saw, at the same moment I'm sure that Obolensky did, a midfield gap in the defensive hedge. So, instead of doing the obvious, Obolensky set course infield for the gap. For a split second it seemed that all the All Blacks ahead of him were frozen there, each on his wrong foot, all realizing that they must now change direction. The black tide swung around but right-wing Obolensky was going like the wind for that part of the goal line that is the left-wing's preserve. Off balance, the defenders clawed at him as he flashed by. Mitchell, on the All Blacks' right wing, went after the unexpected visitor but was beaten by sheer pace. Gilbert essayed the full-backs' traditional cross-field cut-off, but he had started going the wrong way and couldn't catch the long-

striding Russian. Obolensky rounded him, to touch down on the opposite side of the posts from his first try.

Was it in fact the greatest international try of them all? I would cast my vote in favour, because it was something unique – a right-wing wrong-footing all the opposition and running diagonally through them to score a left-winger's try.

Not unlike some routine scores, more than half a century on, by Australia's David Campese, eh? Particularly 'Campissimo's' right-winger's score at the left corner flag, which did for the New Zealanders (again) in the 1991 World Cup semi-final in Dublin. Campese is assured, isn't he, of just about the topmost plinth in the try-scorers' hall of fame?

Mind you, that nicely ruminative old writer on both soccer and cricket A. A. Thomson was not so sure about Obo's flash of lightning. As he noted in his memoir *Rugger My Pleasure*:

Going back nearly thirty years before Obolensky on our time machine, we find older watchers who claim that the most palpitating try they have ever witnessed was scored by K. G. MacLeod against the first touring South African team at Glasgow on 17th November, 1906. Paul Roos's Springboks, a side armed at all points in attack and defence, proved themselves almost as invulnerable as the All Blacks of the previous year, and they lost only their match against Scotland and one other. The late E. D. H. Sewell, in his warm-hearted and delightful *Rugger The Man's Game*, describes almost lyrically an 'impossible' try, scored on a quagmire at Hampden Park, Glasgow, even worse than the morass on which England played Wales at Cardiff at the Arms Park in 1955. The surface was atrocious and the South Africans, temporarily exiled from their own sunny clime, must have thought that they were doomed to grapple with the Highlanders amid their native bogs. The Scottish stand-off half, Munro, taking a pass from his scrum-half, Greig, punted forward to his right and over the head of the Springbok left-wing. On the right wing K. G. MacLeod set off like lightning and took the slimy, greasy ball cleanly while going at absolutely terrific speed on boggy ground, which must have made such speed seem miraculous. As he went on to ground a triumphant try, the volume of applause that arose would have challenged comparison with Hampden's own authentic soccer roar.

Other, slightly less ancient Scots are living still who would claim Wilson Shaw's as the most regal in the royal blue shirt. Their clincher is that it torpedoed England at Twickenham in 1938 – as that diligent and devoted Celtic historian Bryn Thomas dramatically recorded:

It was still anybody's game right up until 2 minutes from the end. Referee Ivor David of Wales, having charge of his first representative match of a long and successful career, looked at his watch. There were just 2 minutes – surely one side or the other would score again! It was Shaw who got the vital score, for he gathered in the loose before any Englishman could kill the ball and went away to the right, dodging and swerving and no one could lay a hand on him. English defenders dived and fell in his weaving path, but none could stop him and eventually he raced round Parker to cross the English line and score the try of the match. Thousands of Scots in the large crowd threw their hats into the air, but they were satisfied now that England could not overhaul Scotland.

After the Second World War, tries came thick and fast for the legend. Schoolboys heard of them at their uncles' knees and then, soon, would be out of short trousers and witnessing the scores of grandeur themselves. 'I know 'cos I was there,' as the sparky Welsh troubadour Max Boyce would sing. The mesmeric Irishman Jack Kyle scored a blinder for the 1950 Lions against the All Blacks at Dunedin. Ditto the French captain Jean Prat against the same side at Colombes four years later. In 1953, for Wales, the Olympic sprinter Ken Jones was famed for a lifetime after his score – from Clem Thomas's cross-kick – against Bob Scott's 1954 All Blacks. (Scores, you see, against the great sides are trebly valued in the memory, and quite right too.)

To be sure, Welshmen had a litany of tries to log off for history. A few, just off the top of my head and without looking up chapter and verse . . . Cliff Morgan's for the Lions at Ellis Park in 1955 (for victory by 23–22) when he put in his place his wing-forward's tormentor of four years before, Basie van Wyk . . . A dozen years later, another young Welshman, Keith Jarrett, making a similar monkey of the staunch English full-back Roger Hosen . . . And utterly great tries too, as memory's rewind button spools back, from the likes in red of Dewi Bebb and J. J. Williams, and Gareth and Phil, and Gerald (the most palpitating of the latter's, a bewildering hopscotch of full-lick sidesteps, was delivered by Davies in the Sam Doble memorial match in 1977). And, of course, Barry John.

Of all his passages of insouciant splendour, in scoring a try Barry's moment of truth came at Wellington on 6 July 1971, for the British Lions against the Combined New Zealand Universities. After about half an hour, there was a set scrum, midfield, on the Universities' 25. The Lions heeled. The reserve scrum-half, the popular Chico Hopkins, shovelled it out to Barry, who caught the ball, stood stock still for a split second, then feinted to drop for goal – the obvious thing. The loose forwards moved in desperately to charge down the 'pot'. Instead, John glided outside their desperate lunge by an inch or two and made as if to link up with his centres, Dawes and Gibson. He 'showed' the next defender the ball, which gave him time to come strongly off his left foot and leave the fellow crash-tackling thin air. Every man jack of the cover was now either on his heels or on precisely the wrong foot, and as four or five of them screeched either to stop, turn or alter gear, like floundering and cursing cartoon cats, John tiptoed delicately through to pop the ball down over the line.

The *Sunday Telegraph* rugby correspondent John Reason, who had seen no end of 'special' tries in his long experience, told his readers the following weekend how every man on either team – not only the mesmerized defenders, who had been turned to stone – had been transfixed in wonder:

> The try on Tuesday left the crowd at Athletic Park absolutely dumbfounded. John had touched the ball down between the posts and was trotting back to take the conversion himself before the realization of what had happened sent the applause crashing round the ground. John confessed afterwards that he thought there must have been an infringement. 'I thought Chico must have put the ball in crooked, or something,' he said. 'I couldn't understand why the crowd was so quiet.'

Many years later, the moment was still vivid for its perpetrator. 'Looking back, I know that try owes a lot to that first feint to drop a goal. To this day I don't know why I didn't go for it, I had enough room to pop it over. But from then on I could just sense intuitively that not one of the opposition around or ahead of me was balanced and sort of ready for me. So I just continued on – outside one, inside the other – all the way to the posts. I know it's funny, but it was all as if I was in a dream, that I had "placed" the defenders exactly where I wanted them, like poles in the garden to practise swerving. I don't know what you call it. Transcendental? Metaphysical? I don't really know the exact definition of those words, but it was just marvellously weird, like I was down there re-enacting the slow-motion replay before the actuality itself had happened. As if I was in a dreamy state of *déjà vu*, that I was in a game, and doing something that had already taken place at another time.'

These general reflections in no way claim to be a definitive listing of all the great tries. Every aficionado has his own stack of favourites that he has seen or heard of. Every country too: any Tongan or Japanese, Canadian, Argentinian, Frenchman or Romanian will have a completely different set of great scores firmly logged in his own rugby culture and legend. Which is how it should be. For instance, any rugger man of a certain age living in Dover could recite at the drop of a red rose the three acknowledged super-duper solo tries indelible in their lore for all time – all at Twickenham: Peter Jackson's against Australia in 1958; and, both against Scotland, Richard Sharp's in 1963 and Andy Hancock's two years later. Applause, applause, and for all three of which Te Deums will be sung for all time. But just twenty miles across the Channel from Dover and a French rugby fan of the same age as likely as not will think simply of Jackson, Sharp and Hancock as possibly an English firm of solicitors. And that same Frenchman would say (to a blank stare from any Brit) that far and away the greatest solo try ever scored was against New Zealand and a 90 m.p.h. gale at Wellington in 1961 by Jean Dupuy. After that he would claim that the three grandest *collectif* tries in all the game's long history were each scored by French teams. Et voila! And he wouldn't be far wrong in that either. In 1994 in New Zealand, France scored a break-out try of utter resplendence to rock the All Blacks terminally. They did the same, against Australia, in the semi-final of the first World Cup in 1987. And in between was Twickenham 1991 and the grandeur of England's Slam but the even greater grandeur of France and Serge Blanco.

The same sort of spent feeling came over all who witnessed the Barbarians' try at Cardiff in 1973. One day, much later, I sat down with the men who scored and said, 'What actually happened?'

> . . . Kirkpatrick . . . to Bryan Williams . . . This is great stuff . . . Phil Bennett covering . . . Chased by Alistair Scown . . . Brilliant . . . Oh, that's brilliant . . . John Williams . . . Pullin . . . John Dawes, great dummy . . . David, Tom David, the half-way line . . . Brilliant, by Quinnell . . . This is Gareth Edwards . . . A dramatic start . . . What a score!

Cliff Morgan's commentary on the Barbarians' try is bound to spool through the minds and hearts of all us nuts. Not Phil Bennett's try really. Not Gareth's. But the Magnificent Seven's. Bennett's was the opening move as he gathered the difficult bobbler under his own posts and, as a furious wave of adrenalin-charged All Blacks bore down on him, in the very act of turning he drove his right foot into not one, not two, but three sidesteps ... Brilliant, oh, that's brilliant ...

'At the time I was intent only on getting out of trouble. I sensed they were right on top of me. Perhaps the whole beautiful, amazing thing would have happened if I hadn't heard Alistair Scown's menacing footsteps bearing down on me. As it was, a bit of a hospital pass I gave to J.P.R., wasn't it?'

... John Williams ...

'Well, certainly I nearly lost my head and Bryan Williams lunged at me. But what utter brilliance by Phil. I remain convinced that the whole thing was really Carwyn James's try. Unique to the Barbarians, who disapproved of coaching, they asked him to give us a talk before the game.

'There was a lot of needle in the game; both we and the All Blacks were treating it as an unofficial fifth Test decider after we [the Lions] had beaten them, coached by Carwyn, down under eighteen months before. Now, before we went out, Carwyn soothed us, calming and relaxed, told us to enjoy it; and I'll never forget his last words, to insist to Phil, who was full of trepidation, hadn't played long for Wales and certainly not for the Lions, to go out and play just like he did for Llanelli.

'So he does, then gives it to me, and as I'm almost scalped I see John [Pullin] outside me, and pop it to him, and do you know I still think to myself sometimes, "Where the heck did he come from? What's John, our trusty old hooker, doing there?"'

... Pullin ...

'Tell him I was there because speedy running forwards are not a new phenomenon. I'd been doing it all my career, but nobody seemed to notice. The try still vivid in my memory? Well, has to be. They seem to replay it every week on TV. Can't escape it. Seriously, there was a real needle to the game. "Exhibition match" was our last thought. A 3–0 win would have been enough for me.

'I suppose, looking back, it would honestly have been normal for me to have kicked for touch when I got the ball but at the time it never entered my mind – I was back in New Zealand playing for Carwyn and the Lions and he drilled us all tour that if someone else had a bit of space then you pass it on to him. And John Dawes was moving quite nicely, wasn't he?'

. . . John Dawes, great dummy . . .

'Ah me, the dummy that never was! But I'm eternally grateful to Cliff, telling the world I was a purveyor of great dummies. And I'm not going to argue with 35 million viewers, am I? In fact I was already looking to put John [Bevan] off down the wing, but the "dummy" was more eyeing the opposition as if I intended to pass. Anyway, suddenly they weren't there any more, I was through the gap and now looking for support inside.

'The fascinating things are: would Benny, who was pretty much a novice in international terms then, have dreamed of opening up if Carwyn's last words hadn't been to "sidestep this lot off the park, like you do at Stradey"; and that Gareth, if you study the TV replay, had covered right back from the half-way to our own line and when John passed to me, Gareth was actually well behind us, so he covered a heck of a lot of ground in that single minute.

'And incidentally, tell old Pullin that if the "mismove" had been invented in 1973, he wouldn't have got his pass and been world famous now.'

. . . David, Tom David, the half-way line . . .

'Is that really me, taking the ball at such a helter-skelter in every one of those million TV replays? I wish the BBC would stop them. Well, the world and his wife thinks I'm still twenty-three and an electric athlete of under fourteen stone, and then they see my middle-aged spread coming through the door and say: "That's never him, the guy in the Baa-Baas try – can't be, impossible."

'No, actually, whenever I see it I think of two blokes from Gloucester way. Well, of course, I had only been told I was replacing the injured Mervyn [Davies] on the day of the match. Hadn't played for three weeks seriously because of my knee, see. The Saturday before, I thought I needed a run-out to get a bit fit, so asked some pals up at Cilfynydd for a game.

'They were playing a little club at Gloucester called Hucclecote. No problem, they say, so off we go to Gloucester and I turn out in the centre. Foggy, I remember, which is perhaps the reason that I seem to score a try every time I get the ball. Tons of them, haring through the centre just like that. Great. Knee great too, so no worries by the end of the week when I'm called up for the Baa-Baas.

'Except little me's surrounded by all these all-time greats. The only sadness is, I'm not in the programme, being such a late call-up. It also worried two blokes in the great crowd, too. They were from Hucclecote. It said "Mervyn Davies" in the programme. They must have thought they'd either had too many beers or were in the middle of a bad dream. "Stone me, if that's not the bugger who played in the centre for Cilfynydd against us last Saturday."

'That evening they sought me out to settle their argument. "Hello, boys," I said. "Sure, I'm the local valley boy from the centre for Cilfynydd who made good in a week, and gave the pass for Derek Quinnell's magnificent catch this very afternoon."'

. . . Brilliant, by Quinnell . . .

'Funny you describe it as a slip-catch on the run. That very thing, ridiculously, was going through my mind as I held it. That there

I was on the Arms Park, and I was thinking about a boyhood triumph all those years ago at Coleshill Sec. Mod. when my Form 2A played the big boys from 4A in the school cricket cup final and I took a truly wonderful catch at silly mid-on, just like this one I had just taken off Tom. And I'm pretty certain that childhood winning catch was off the bowling of Form 2A's little Phil Bennett himself.

'When we got back with the cup that afternoon our form master, Mr Brace, said, "Quinnell, a truly magnificent, magnificent catch, but remember you only field at silly mid-on because you're built for comfort, not speed." That's what I was thinking as I scooped up Tom's pass at my bootlaces – till I was soon enough exploded out of my reverie by this series of banshee shouts behind me.

'I knew Gareth was coming up like a train, screaming for the ball like a raving idiot – jeepers, what a din. So recalling Mr Brace again and my lack of speed, I just pop the ball out to the left and let John [Bevan] and Gareth sort out who takes the pass. I guessed it would be Gareth, mind you, for he wanted something to show for having run so far so fast, which was not his usual practice if he could help it, was it?'

. . . This is Gareth Edwards . . . a dramatic start . . .

When they talk about it, Derek will chaff Gareth that he was only allowed to make his name for posterity thanks to Quinnell's 'magnificent unselfishness, when he could easily have run in the ball himself'. In fact, Edwards had to pin his ears back and go like fury to catapult in at the corner. Typically, he says it was 'a privilege to finish such a move'.

. . . What a score! . . .

In the grandstand, the game's eminence, seventy-five-year-old Lord Wakefield of Kendal, turned and shook hands with the Barbarians' celebrated president, Herbert Waddell, and whispered in his ear: 'My friend, I will now die a happy man.'

Meanwhile, not far away from the two old men, Carwyn James took a deep, satisfied pull on his Senior Service and smiled his private, contented smile. I rang him up and asked him to write, for the *Guardian*, of the moment, rare and unforgettable, when you can play at a level outside the conscious; when everything is instinctive, but as clear as a bell because you have practised it so often and, especially, dreamed it – that unique moment when sport not only achieves but assumes an art form.

There have been three great 'collective' tries logged by history. I saw them all. I was there on 21 May 1980 in Potchefstroom's quaint little low-slung grandstand. This time, the estimable Quinnell himself was producer-director. High on the veldt, the sun was dropping and time was fast running out for the beleaguered British: 16–19, and it was going to be the Lions' first defeat outside Tests in South Africa in eight years and twenty-six matches. The referee, as the football commentator once put it, 'was looking at his whistle and preparing to blow his watch'. The frantic counter-attacking wave came and came again as the ball went through thirty-three pairs of hands in a move lasting one minute and thirty-six seconds – an unbelievable amount of time, if you think about it.

On and on it went, from hand to hand, from left to right, forwards and backwards, forwards and backwards and forwards again ... Quinnell always there, rucking and running alongside his tiny West Walian lieutenant, Richards. It was almost touch rugby. O'Driscoll, Williams, Rees and Phillips; Patterson, with the fast fingers, kept switching the options; cool-hand Renwick was always there, and the pacing Woodward. What started as a rather forlorn gesture of defiance – the referee could not blow the final whistle till the ball was dead – rolled on and on to a crescendo of heroic proportions, as the doughty Scot called Hay turned into a tackle on the touchline only a few feet away from me, to show the spring-heeled Slemen a gap, through which he drove the killing, thrilling thrust.

Pandemonium – and 50,000 South African hands smacked palm-to-palm in generosity and wonder. The old Empire came together again for just a fleeting moment or two.

The third try, in March 1991, might, in all truth, have been the best. Well, context is all. This, by France and inspired by Serge Blanco, was run in during the intensity of a Grand Slam finale. Grandeur, it was. England missed a long penalty and all eyes and senses, certainly those of the England XV for a fatal moment, relaxed and prepared for a 22 drop-out.

Suddenly all hell broke loose – or, rather, the incomparable Serge Blanco, dusky warrior-captain of France, did. '*Moi, moi*,' he shouted to Berbizier, who fielded the ball. Blanco has always put his trust in gods who favour the foolhardy. He was now across his line but still 10 yards short of his own 22. In a trice the ball was with Lafond outside him and the wing's left hip took out Andrew, first to spot the danger; an instantaneous finger-tip pass inside allowed Sella, at speed, to round his own despairing white marker.

Sella was over the 22 and momentarily clear as England re-grouped and frantically funnelled back. The stalwart Probyn had tanked across to confront him on France's 10-yard line. Sella feinted to knife inside him, so stopping the prop in his tracks, and, as he did so, he turned in a dummy-scissors loop and fed on the outside again the delicate Camberabero. The pit-a-pat fly-half could now snipe across the half-way mark.

Then, with dainty exactness, he chipped the ball over the head of the retreating Hodgkinson, caught it full pelt in his stride and was now up to England's 22. Though England's bold general Carling had, remarkably, made it across the field, he could only fling himself at Camberabero a split second after the Frenchman had dapped the most perfectly weighted cross-kick to within 5 yards of the posts.

This took out the corner-flagging Hill and left Saint-André to compose himself, collect and triumphantly launch himself at the line as Guscott's all-in, last-gasp dive lassoed his ankles. The palpitating thing was done. *Et voilà*.

Sucking a Lemon

MIKE SEABROOK

One of the more amusing by-products of modern methods of packaging sport and sportsmen is the 'biographies' of young men whose lives can scarcely be said to have properly begun. There have been, it is true, men for whom one might argue a case for a biography, or at least a first volume, while they were still in their twenties: Alexander of Macedon and the younger Pitt, certainly; Byron and Marlowe, yes; Marco Polo; maybe Mendelssohn. As far as I know none of these was honoured with a biography during his twenties. Steve Davis and Graeme Hick, however, to mention only the first two to come to mind, were. But Will Carling, captain of the current England rugby football XV, has been the subject of *two*, one authorized and friendly, the other rather less so.

I read the authorized version, and formed an impression of a conventional young man, with a normal human ration of virtues and weaknesses, strengths and failings, exceptional only for his prowess as a rugby player; and – meaning him no disrespect – the story of his short life to date I found of little interest.

There was, however, much in the book that *was* of interest, including the account of the continuous antagonism, which gradually built up to open hostility over the last few years, between the players of the England team and the rugby establishment as represented by the Rugby Football Union based at Twickenham. The resentment flared up over various issues and pretexts, but the root cause was usually the same: the vexed question of whether, and to what extent, the game of rugby union should turn professional.

In the end the question was resolved with almost brutal swiftness, which made one wonder quite how it had managed to generate such endlessly protracted schism and debate in the first place. Along came big, beaming Uncle Kerry (with Rupert Murdoch skulking in the shadows behind him, like a ruffian on the stair in a Victorian melodrama); a quick reprise of the sleight-of-hand act he did on cricket's overlords a few years ago, and, behold, the game was professional. Just like that – as if all the agonizing and the tears, all the ferocious protestations of the RFU that the change would come over their dead bodies, and the gathering bitterness between them and the players, had never been.

It had to come, of course. The demands made of the players were becoming ever heavier. In part this was only an increased requirement for full physical fitness. But the mental and psychological pressures of the game were becoming increasingly heavy also. The pressures of being the best, and of representing their countries, in a competitive game, were also growing more and more intense. The attentions of the press are ever more intrusive and, some would say, impertinent; and perhaps most potent of all, the expectations of the paying spectators are rising to new heights all the time.

In this last particular the England players might be said to have been victims of their own success. The early 1990s were not especially bright years for English sport. The international football side failed to win a European Championship that they were widely expected to win, and then failed to gain a place in the final stages of the 1994 World Cup in the United States. As usual in an age when someone must be blamed for everything that happens, a sacrificial victim was sought, found and persecuted, and Graham Taylor, the most intelligent, thoughtful and articulate England manager in years, resigned in what the press, at least, chose to proclaim as disgrace. Meanwhile the England Test cricket side continued bumping along the rocky bottom of international cricket that had been their all-too-familiar habitat for some years.

The triumphant rugby side was therefore a brilliant new constellation in an otherwise rather gloomy sporting sky. They should have won the Five Nations Championship in 1990, having it denied them by defeat by Scotland as a result of an unfortunate misjudgement in the final match of the championship. In 1991, however, they made no mistake, and won the Grand Slam, and right handsomely. They repeated the achievement in 1992, and in between came a more than creditable second in the World Cup. In 1995 they won the Grand Slam for yet a third time, including in the performance a victory over France which in the view of many was the finest performance by an England side in living memory; and in the third World Cup in South Africa they took a fourth place that was more than respectable in the context - the context being a generally rather ill-starred tour, in difficult conditions, both physical and artificially created.

All this had raised rugby enormously in the public consciousness; and the new appetite for the game was accentuated by the dismal showing of the representative sides in other popular sports. But the acquisition of a vast and vastly enthusiastic new public is a mixed blessing.

As a spectator game, rugby probably comes somewhere between association football and cricket. Football is a natural game for spectators: it is fast, graceful yet tough, requiring, and at its best demonstrating, a heady mixture of athleticism, speed, aggression, power and skill; but it is also, and this is the essence of it, very simple in concept and – notwithstanding the prodigious skills of the players – in its execution also. (C.f. Ronald Reagan: 'It ain't easy, but it sure is simple.')

Cricket too is a game of much grace and skill. It presents difficulties as a game for the spectator, however, not least in that the action all takes place so far from the spectator that he is simply unable to see most of the more subtle things that go on on the pitch. It is also somewhat handicapped by having an extremely complicated set of laws, often bewildering to the players, let alone the spectators.

Rugby can be as fast, exciting and simple as football, but in general it is less so. It is not as subtle as cricket, or as fully rounded; but that is not to say that it is without subtlety, or delicacy or grace.

And there can be few more majestic and exhilarating sights in all sport than a rugby side sweeping inexorably down a field, the ball swung along the back line in a series of long, low, raking passes at breakneck speed; the heroic tackle, the ball hurled over his head by the falling centre; the sheer, awesome power of some colossus of a second-row forward as he bursts through the clutching arms of the defence, like a man suddenly bursting the confining bonds of a strait-jacket, and the final salmon-leap as the wing-threequarter sails in a great arc through the air and makes his try in the corner with a split second to spare.

That is only one imagined example. Countless moments like it will come bubbling up to the surface of any rugby devotee's memory at will. He has only to close his eyes and whole pageants of bravery, even heroism, grace and nerve-tingling excitement will unreel before the vivid mind's eye of memory. The 1995 World Cup produced a bounteous quantity of exciting and exhilarating rugby. But . . .

. . . but there are ways in which rugby is closer to cricket than to football, ways in which it is beyond the grasp of most mere spectators. For rugby, too, has its subtleties – some of them, notably those carried on between more or less consenting adults in the privacy of the scrum, of a kind that the game might not wish to boast about. Rugby also shares with cricket a highly complex set of laws, and they are known thoroughly by, one guesses, about the same percentage of rugby devotees as in cricket. I have yet to find anyone standing at a rugby match who can give me a satisfactory explanation of the off-side law. I watch my local (and excellent) side at Pontarlier (watch for them in the French first division some time very soon) with a group of a dozen or so friends, and I should estimate that in the average game something like 30 per cent of the referee's decisions are for reasons we can't work out – and most of us have played rugby at a respectable club standard. The reason, in many cases, is simple enough: we aren't close enough to see what has gone on.

None of this is anything like sufficient reason to suggest that rugby should not be regarded as a game for spectators. Nor do I feel that the *fact* of the passive but paying spectator need have any deleterious effect on the game. It may, indeed, have a beneficial one. The spectators clearly want to see more tries and less kicking. So do I. The spectators, apparently, feel that too many games are won and lost on penalties. So do I. The result of this, with any luck, will be sufficient pressure on the law-making authorities to get the penalty replaced by the free kick for many of the less serious offences for which penalties are currently awarded.

Better still, it is likely that it will be spectator power, more than anything else, that will put pressure on the rugby authorities to insist on a greater degree of uniformity among referees in their interpretation and enforcement of the laws. This aspect of the game is at present in a highly unsatisfactory state: the players are entitled to know, at least as precisely as a dynamic game such as rugby permits, where they stand under the laws and *vis-à-vis* the referee; and at the moment they don't. Conduct which one referee will view as near-criminal and penalize ferociously the next may smile at as nothing more than youthful high spirits. In particular there is an apparent difference in perception of many of the most crucial laws of the game between referees from the northern and southern hemispheres which is making matches between sides from opposite halves of the world more and more fraught, rather as if two nuclear arms reduction negotiators were speaking through an interpreter who understood the language of only one of them.

If, therefore, the only thing to be feared from the influence of spectators was a coarsening effect (such as it has already had on cricket), I should dismiss the fear as unfounded. Unfortunately, the passive spectator culture is almost certain to introduce something else, altogether less welcome, into the game.

For the true sportsman, the result of the match is almost incidental – almost but never quite, which makes all the difference. This is not to say that any sportsman should be indifferent to the result of his game: on the contrary, no one should ever set foot on a rugby field who is not determined to win by all legal and fair means.

But it is fair to say that the maxim of the real sportsman is that wanting to win is everything, but winning itself is nothing. Nothing could be much further from the truth, however, as far as the spectator culture is concerned; the passive spectator, having nothing invested in the game but his money, has only one thing to want and to wait for: results. Success, success and more success are the only yardsticks available by which the spectator can measure whether he has received value for his money. The ultimate effects of this have already been seen in soccer. That such notions fly in the face of the whole principle of amateurism, with its emphasis on sportsmanship, a modified form of chivalry, and the notion of 'May the better team win', is self-evident, and is the clearest indication of the divide between the players at international level and the RFU establishment and its satellite bodies, with their fiercely protective sentiments towards the amateur spirit. If you further complicate matters by allowing big business to get its foot in the door, you allow a second rogue factor into an equation that was not made to hold even one. Rugby cannot serve two masters any more than anyone or anything else. *A fortiori*, it can't serve three.

This, and the spectator culture in general, has had an even more dismaying consequence: the creation of the kind of false loyalty, both specious and pernicious, that says 'my country, right or wrong'. This, too, I suspect, was central to the bitter divisions between the players and the establishment.

Patriotism is among the most contemptible of vices: a means by which demagogues and psychopaths get to fight to the last drop of other people's blood. They take their fellow citizens' love of their country and use it to dazzle and mesmerize them into a willingness to go forth and risk being butchered for a slogan on a banner. Love of country itself is, in any case, surely the last distillation of arrogance: 'I love this country, because *I* was born there.' And while I don't say that the massed choirs bawling their tuneless rendering of 'Swing Low, Sweet Chariot' at Twickenham are to be considered on a par with martial music and calls to arms, I do, none the less, loathe massed chanting and singing at sporting events. They call up inescapable associations: of mass hysteria; of Nuremberg rallies, lynching parties and a crowd baying 'Barabbas'.

I suggested that this was the root cause of the divisions between the players and the RFU. The reason is that in this matter the players appear to have taken sides. In the biography of Will Carling I mentioned, he is quoted at one point as saying: 'They [the Twickenham crowd] have come over to our side. It used to be fairly dead. *The fans were there to watch rugby, not to support England.* Now they have the same pride as us [my italics]. It is clear from the context that Carling regards this as desirable, and I don't think it is presuming too far to take it that this represents the view of other players as well. I suspect also that such a view would be anathema to the RFU; and if those are the two polarized views, on this I am emphatically on the side of the establishment.

The players evidently like and respond to thunderous chanting, singing and roaring in support, and they're entitled to their preferences. So are the crowd entitled to theirs. As it happens, large numbers of the Twickenham crowd agree with the players, so, alas, I seem to be outvoted. Fair enough; but equally, I'm entitled to *my* preferences, too. And I think watching rugby is what the crowd ought to be at Twickenham to do. For me, merely supporting one side of a sporting encounter is a very poor justification – the poorest – for going to the match. If that's why you go to watch rugby matches – or any other sport – you're likely to spend half your time feeling miserable and disappointed. There are two sides out there, both of them trying to win, and generally only one of them can do so.

Really, this ought to be the most self-evident truism; but most people seem to have lost sight of it. I don't think we do losers anything like the honour, even reverence, that they deserve. It ought not to need pointing out that it is integral to the whole concept of games that someone must lose. Without a loser there can be no winner. Losers are exactly as important as winners: not more, not less, but precisely, mathematically, equal. If you can't face the possibility of losing – and more, if you can't face that possibility *with equanimity*, you shouldn't be involved in games, because you don't understand the concept.

This is all part of a larger phenomenon, a besetting vice of our time: that of hysteria, of hyperbole, in general of taking things too seriously. At one point in the biography of Carling, the author quotes the Secretary of the Scottish Rugby Union, Bill Hogg, as remarking that the price on the black market for a pair of tickets for the Scotland–England match – £1,000 – was 'entirely out of proportion for a rugby match'. There is an unmistakable note of disagreement, even disapproval, in the tone of the author's reference to this. Yet it seems to me to be a perfectly sensible comment to make. We ought not to shrink from declaring that a thing is not worth more than a certain amount, even if there happens to be a buyer who is a billionaire and capable of paying the price demanded. So, for instance, no bottle of wine on earth is worth £500, no car a quarter of a million. And no pair of tickets to a sporting event is worth anything approaching a thousand pounds, even if the potential buyer is the Sheikh of all the Arabias.

Games are games: that, and no more. A game is, by any dictionary definition, a pleasure, a pastime, a way of relaxing and enjoying oneself, a respite from the everyday drudgery of work. Games are not war, or a substitute for war, despite the best efforts of every dictator and political psychopath in history to elevate them there in the absence of a real war with real soldiers to play with. When overheated sports writers start comparing games of rugby or anything else with battles in wars, and the feelings of beaten teams with those of grieving bereaved, as Carling's biographer does a little later in the same passage, it's time for someone to jolt them out of such intellectual slovenliness. I don't mean one has to be po-faced about it; but they shouldn't be allowed to get away with debasing the currency of language and foisting their vulgar, primary-colour world view on more temperate people.

Games are of considerable value in relieving the lives of quiet desperation that most people are obliged to lead, and in allowing us to forget work for a bit, but they are not very *important* – except to those who depend on them for their livelihood. We shouldn't let this heavily interested group rob us of our objectivity by lulling us into thinking that games are as important to us as they are to them. And it follows from this that if games are not very important, neither are games players. As far as money is concerned, they are of course entitled to get as much as they can. But if the day should ever come when people's survival is assessed by how essential they are, games players will immediately find themselves dispensable.

Rugby players will do well to remember this even as they begin to reap extravagant benefits from their game. In view of the great gulf between the players and the RFU in attitudes towards the game, this is one reason why it is a good thing that most of the players have chosen, in the end, to remain under the auspices of the existing controlling bodies, rather than deserting to the likes of Packer and Murdoch. The continuing presence of men with an older-fashioned, less money-orientated philosophy may, with luck, help to retain a sense of proportion as the pace of change accelerates.

There are times, though, when the RFU try their supporters sorely – when, to adapt Orwell, their worst advertisement is their members.

Thus in 1995, ten days before the England party were to set off for South Africa and the best chance, probably, that an England side ever had of winning the World Cup, the RFU chose to dismiss Carling from the captaincy for the moral equivalent of eating peas off his knife. On a television interview he fell for the old dodge of leaving the microphone on when he thought he was off the air, and described the RFU Committee as 'fifty-seven old farts'. For *this* he was deprived of the captaincy – at the very moment when the damage done to the England team, their morale, their chances, their supporters and their country could hardly have been greater.

Admittedly he was reinstated twenty-four hours later, after furious demonstrations of public outrage and after Rob Andrew and

Dean Richards had put a gun to the RFU's head by making it clear that they would refuse the captaincy if offered it. How the RFU could have imagined so stiff-necked and spiteful an act of private revenge could succeed, when the only sensible response would have been to laugh sportingly and ignore Carling's gaffe for the inconsequential trifle it was, is beyond normal understanding. The only real consequence of this ridiculous affair was that RFU fellow travellers concluded that Carling's description of the governing body had been only too accurate.

Whether this extraordinary piece of over-reaction by the RFU actually did in the end have any effect on the performance in South Africa of the England players it is difficult to say. Certainly in their opening games they did not seem to have settled down: they were ill at ease, their play was constipated and lack-lustre, and they were more than a little lucky not to be defeated by Argentina and even the minnows of Italy. On the other hand, in the quarter-final they avenged themselves on Australia in a performance that was highly spirited, if not the last word in elegance. But then, England's winning rugby over the last few years has never been elegant: it has always been left to the French, the All Blacks and the Australians to produce flowing grace and flair. England have tended to be more solid and stolid. Nothing wrong with this: it's a matter of national characteristics; the English have always preferred suet pud to a lighter-than-air madeleine.

England's real débâcle came in their semi-final against the All Blacks; and that match also, as it happens, provides a first-class example of the absurd hyperbole of which I spoke earlier; and it was an example, too, of how the world's press so often speak with a unanimous voice, and unanimously get it all wrong.

To listen to the world's press after this semi-final, you would have thought not so much that there was only one team out there playing, but that there was only one player on the field, performing prodigies all on his own. The adulation heaped upon Jonah Lomu would have been out of place in response to the Second Coming; as a comment on the performance of one member of a team of fifteen who, on the day, all played exceptionally well, its main effect was to insult the other members of that team while losing all substance as a compliment to Lomu himself.

The reality of the match was totally lost in the tidal waves of hyperbole on Lomu. The truth was that in the second half England not only outscored New Zealand but outplayed them, producing the most ferocious 40 minutes' rugby I have seen ever. The truest tribute to the extraordinary quality of their opponents that day is that they restricted England's scoring in that explosive forty minutes to twenty-six points, and scored twenty themselves, so keeping the winning margin they had set up in the opening ten minutes of the match. Any other rugby side would have been annihilated against the ferocity of that half from England, and no amount of first-half lead would have sufficed. As it was, the All Blacks won by taking England utterly by surprise in those first ten minutes. Some might suggest that the All Blacks took it a little easier in the second half, starting it as they did thirty points up. But not only does this fly in the face of the observable reality, not only is it at odds with everything we have known about New Zealand rugby over a century or more; much more to the point, a team ruthless enough to pile up 145 points against Japan is somewhat less than likely to let up and ease the pressure against the one side that all the former imperial possessions like to thrash out of sight if they can.

But to claim that Lomu more or less wiped out England on his own is a travesty of the truth. The absurdity of this was brutally rammed home in the final, when Lomu, in particular, was made to look distinctly ordinary by the South Africans, mainly by the expedient of not being respecters of persons or being intimidated by reputations. They played it simple, and they got it right: when Lomu got the ball, they got Lomu. They tackled him fairly, but they tackled him instantly and very, very hard; and he didn't do a thing in the match.

None of this is to take anything away from Lomu's real merits: his four tries against England were all splendid to behold – though it's worth mentioning that none of them was any better than the one scored against England by Emile Ntamack in the third-place play-off. Indeed, to my mind, that was the best try against England of all, a piece of pure magic such as only the French seem able to conjure up. Ntamack's try was a thing of ethereal grace, a swerving, ducking, weaving glide, like a gazelle, whereas Lomu's usual approach is more reminiscent of an armoured column.

The truth is, of course, that Lomu is a player of prodigious talents, a little raw and green at the moment, but one who is destined to thrill the coming generation of rugby spectators, now that he has committed himself to the New Zealand RFU and resisted the blandishments of Rugby League, Packer and Murdoch.

Which brings us back to the question of professionalism. It is worth contemplating what effect the switch, so sudden and dramatic after such an interminable period of phoney war, will have. Will it ultimately turn out to be for the good of the game? Will it, as the more empurpled traditionalists are no doubt fearing, be the beginning of the end of rugby as we know it – as dyed-in-the-wool cricket purists could claim has happened in their game as a result of all the changes brought about in recent years? Or will it all prove to have been the most enormous storm in a teacup, with the game going on much as it has before?

My own feelings incline towards the last of the three possibilities. There may even be a certain amount of streamling of the game – some simplification of the rules, perhaps, – which would not be by any means a bad thing. As far as the mere introduction of money into the game is concerned, there is certainly much less cause for alarm now that Packer and Murdoch will not be wielding their influence.

All the same, the people in charge of the game should be on their toes as the new dawn rises. If they are worried about the effect the introduction of big money will have on their beloved game, they have good reason. For a start, where big money is found, big business is sure to come sniffing round close behind. And big business is a dangerous playmate. For when a game invites business into its parlour, it risks doing two things: first, it puts the game in the position of acting as a stalking horse for big business in its constant campaign to evade paying tax; and second, it puts the game in hock to hard-faced men who will run rings round the people who run rugby. There will be over-exposure, exploitation, vulgarization and, in the end, when rugby has served its turn, there will be callous abandonment when some new and glossier vehicle has been found to replace it. Rugby will do well to remember that in the cold, hard world that will be pitching camp on the fair turf of Twickenham there is no such thing as a free lunch.

If anyone is to act as watchdog to keep the more ostentatious and vulgar consequences of commercialism at bay, who better to do the job than the old official controlling bodies? And if we want reassurance that they will do it well, there is already reason for optimism in the calm and sensible way in which, for example, the domestic clubs have been guided into the changeover to professionalism.

All this is a long way from the happiest associations that rugby has for me. My playing career was spectacularly undistinguished. However, I enjoyed barging about and using my considerable weight, in a lumpen sort of way, at loose-head. And later on I found that even if I did play the game like an ox on an ice-rink, there was still room for a substantial contribution for a drinker of my abilities in the clubhouse afterwards; I also enjoyed singing all the daft rude songs in the bath, on the bus home and in the bar, and I regret the passing of that kind of ambience at rugby matches. People take their pleasures too seriously these days, and the world is a drabber place for it.

Still, I enjoy watching the game even now. For me this has always brought up images of standing, perished, leaning into a biting wind, at somewhere like Exmouth, or Holt or North Walsham, or Old Deer Park, watching London Welsh, so sadly diminished for the moment, and, now, Pontarlier. I'd like to go to at least one big match, preferably between England and France, where I could enjoy the sensation of pleasantly divided loyalties, but I know that it would make no difference to my natural inclination towards things on a smaller, more intimate scale. I like the sensation of being so close to the action that one can actually hear the crunch of bone on bone in the tackles, and see the loose-head's eyes water (and hear what he says) when the opposing lock wields a sly boot in the scrum. I like being able to amble round the ground, selecting the most advantageous position, and passing the time of day with any friends I might bump into. Most of all I like being able to drift into the clubhouse after the game and stand with a beer and jaw with the players and other friends. I suppose what it amounts to is that if I must perforce be a spectator I will at least try to be as unpassive as I can. I expect to be still doing it long after the absurd professional–amateur wrangle is ancient history.

The Ten Commandments of Touring

DAMIAN HOPLEY

As rugby union increasingly finds itself in the clutches of endless modification, both on and off the pitch, as professionalism begins to infiltrate and administrators worldwide struggle to preserve the very foundations of the game, there is one truly Corinthian bastion of rugby that must surely remain unscathed: the tour.

Following his much-publicized disregard for the rules of football back in 1823, William Webb Ellis would have had no idea of the true extent of his misdemeanour in that hotel owners throughout the world would one day curse his disciples. Indeed, within a few years of Webb Ellis picking up the ball and running with it, the master-in-charge of games at Rugby School was probably beseeching Dr Arnold for funds to subsidize an exotic trip abroad – doubtless selling it as fifteen evangelicals spreading their own particular brand of 'muscular Christianity'.

Before going any further I should clarify a few popular misconceptions that always arise when a tour is mooted. First and foremost, a tour is most definitely not a holiday. While many of you may struggle to convince kith and kin otherwise, a holiday and a tour are two completely separate entities, best explained by this brief example. I would not, for instance, travel to Hong Kong at the end of March in the hope of getting away from it all, looking for a few days to put my feet up. Similarly, I could think of nothing more absurd than travelling with thirty 'lads' to a secluded beach in the Caribbean for a relaxing fortnight.

In this essay I shall delve into the composition of a 'successful' tour – the attitudes of the tourists, their destinations, and the unsuspecting hosts. At its conclusion we shall be no closer to a tried and tested formula but, with the aid of my somewhat limited experience, we will have a rough guide to help the non-rugby-tourist understand what all the fuss is about.

What makes a 'successful' rugby tour? Sadly, the primary concern is inevitably money. Unfortunately not every club has a wealthy committee member willing to dig deep and throw a few coppers in the kitty for the 'chaps' to 'head orf' to 'Honkers' for a week's jolly. Begging letters are penned, numerous fund-raising events are initiated and distant members of the family hear from their long-lost rugby-playing relatives for the first time in years.

Of fund-raising events, one of the tried and tested perennials is a sporting dinner. Once a quality guest speaker has been collared (there can be nothing more excruciating than listening to some drunken old fool rant on about his winning drop goal in the Somerset Cup final of 1922), the next crucial item is the auction of sporting memorabilia. The timing of this is critical and, as a rule of thumb, the later in the evening it is left the better. Just as the cheap house red begins to take its toll so should the first item come under the hammer. Needless to say, the more legless the punters, the more they will pay up for what are usually items that have lost all their appeal by morning. Only recently at the Harlequins' City Dinner one of the guests paid £8,000 for a weekend's trip to Johannesburg to watch the rugby World Cup final. I trust his wife was delighted by the news.

Once sufficient funds have been gathered, the crucial decision to be made is the destination of the tour. This is usually best taken by a small nucleus of senior players and committee, with the possibilities being put to the vote. The club, however, must take stock of the aims of the tour. Is it intended to be: developmental; an end-of-season knees-up; or simply an excuse to escape from the strains of everyday life?

If it is to be a developmental tour then the destination is all-important. When one has the task of bringing on up-and-coming talent in the game – something at which the English are notoriously poor – then one must gauge the talent within the side. On the back end of a poor domestic season it would be ludicrous to head off to the South of France with a group of under-19s to play friendlies against teams such as Biarritz or Bègles. Rest assured that when the opposition appear questions will be asked not only as to their dates of birth but also their genetic heritage. Things will be made no clearer when, at the post-match function, as you down your third gallon of Pernod and finish your second bowl of pâté, your opposite number introduces you to his wife and ten-year-old son. Beware of developmental tours: insist that the referee checks both studs and birth certificates before kick-off. Take a large playing squad – they will all get games by fair means or foul – and advise the manager and coach to pack their boots and a copy of the Queensberry Rules just in case of emergency.

At the other end of the spectrum is the end-of-season jolly to celebrate the club's survival in the league. Assuming that the kitty is brimming with cash, the more exotic destinations may be pursued. Despite my previous comments on the absurdity of taking a rugby team for an idyllic week on the beach, I have to admit that there is undoubtedly a method in that madness.

Some of the best venues to which I have travelled are sun-drenched beaches where the standard of rugby, although relatively poor, is more than compensated for by the standard of living. A prime example is Bermuda, where the hospitality is legendary. Of paramount importance in any destination is the accommodation. If you are lucky enough to be 'billeted', you get more of a feel for the country and its people. Despite the apparent glamour of touring with an international side, it can be a very isolated existence, wherein the only thing you see of the country is a hotel room, a couple of bars and a lot of rugby pitches (though in which order depends very much on the individual . . .). I am in constant awe of people who are good enough to host rugby players from foreign climes. Knowing the rugby beast as I do, the last place I would want him would be in my home.

Assuming that the club has chosen their destination, the next step should be to look at the creeds, cultures and customs that the tourists might face. In using a religious connotation, I like to think of tours as a form of pilgrimage and when the two are compared there are striking similarities – such as uniformity in dress codes, the chanting of familiar songs and the sense of community and fellowship throughout – one of the few differences being that while a trip to Lourdes could miraculously culminate in the cure of an ailment, an international weekend in Dublin will inevitably result in a rapid decline in health. As with a pilgrimage to the Holy Land, a tour requires a respect for local cultures and customs – in other words, the opposite of the much-publicized antics of Wasps RFC in the Cobra Tens in Malaysia in 1992, where in the heat of the midday sun they bared their finest assets for the world to see. Hardly surprising that in a Muslim country this cheeky behaviour was frowned upon and the Kuala Lumpur Five were landed with severe fines and an order to leave the country forthwith. The following year the competitors were each issued with a list of dos and don'ts and the liaison officers breathed a sigh of relief as the tournament went off without so much as a bare shoulder.

If the tour is lucky enough to be travelling to the South Sea Islands, and Fiji in particular, they will be treated to a welcome like no other in the world. When England toured there in 1991 we had the considerable privilege of staying in the Nandi Sheraton, one of the most beautiful hotels I have been fortunate enough to stay in. On arrival we were invited to a traditional *kava* ceremony. The elders of the tribe sit round a large wooden mixing bowl in which tree roots are washed in a muddy concoction. A small bowl containing the muddy waters is then passed round the group, who are also seated. Before receiving the bowl and drinking, one must clap three times to ward off the evil spirits and then drink the potion. While the taste takes some getting used to, one soon experiences a warm glow all over and the world seems a better place. The secret of *kava* is that it is not alcohol-based, as is widely assumed, but is actually a narcotic. When you get up to go, after a few bowls of the stuff, you find your legs have ceased to function – much to the amusement of your hosts. Next night we got our revenge by sending our hosts off to the local Guinness bar with Messrs Rendall and Leonard. We're eagerly awaiting the rematch.

Once on the pitch the Fijians are a different beast. Rugby has been a way of life in Fiji since colonial times, and there can be no more awe-inspiring sight than watching these wonderfully athletic players perform their mercurial ball skills in full flight. As we have seen increasingly, the islanders have also perfected the spear tackle. The safest place to be is in the stand.

On the tour the midweek XV played against Fiji B in Nandi and one of the main concerns was self-preservation. The game had been relatively quiet until Ian Hunter, of Northampton and British Lions fame, was set on a short ball careering towards the Fijian midfield. From out of nowhere one of the opposition centres hoisted a straight arm and almost took poor Hunter's head off. As the home crowd whooped their approval the centre – obviously a keen amateur cricketer in his spare time – simply bowed his head and walked from the pitch *à la* Desmond Haynes, realizing that he would not be troubling the scorers any more. The early bath was not so much calling as screaming.

The following morning, the Test side was announced to play Fiji and, inevitably, some members of the midweek team were aggrieved at their omission. The 'bitter and twisted' minority called its inaugural meeting of the tour at 6.30 p.m. sharp in the cocktail bar. One of the worries of being dropped or left out of a side is that the casualties will lose all interest and go 'off' tour. Judgement becomes seriously warped as a player feels the world is against him.

At the preordained time the '6 + 1' club (or the Silver Bullets, as they are affectionately known) gathered and, within no time, the cocktails were flowing, the knives were being sharpened and the banter flew about the players in the Test team as the atmosphere livened up. A tremendous sense of commitment was developing between the players, fortified by frequent visits to the bar. This was becoming a potentially explosive situation.

As the night drew on, the karaoke bar beckoned and we discovered with considerable glee that Geoff Cooke, the honorary manager of the England team, had divulged his room number to one of the boys, telling him to put a *few* drinks on his tab, if needs be . . . No second invitation was needed. Not a soul in the bar was allowed to pay for a drink that evening. The barmen ably assisted us by signing as Mr Cooke throughout the night and the party went off with a bang. The wheels had, for a brief while, well and truly come off. With the midweek skipper, John Olver, leading the troops from the front with the now legendary cry of 'Shooters?' every five minutes as he produced yet another tequila, the bar was rocking. Come 2.30 a.m., as proceedings drew to a close, we were in no mood to stop the frenzy, so off we went into the night looking for mischief.

As we entered the outside bar we noticed that the band had vacated the stage and, somewhat foolishly (how I rue that day), I let it be known that I could thrash out a tune to a 'sing-along-a-Bobby-Crush' standard. No sooner said than we were up on the stage trying to get the instruments and the speakers connected for an impromptu gig. The security guards were shooed away as we convinced them that we had years of experience on the road and that this was just another venue on our world tour.

It was left to our roadie – Nigel Redman, a sparks by trade – to flick the switch and send us out live, all over the resort. We had Dewi 'Ringo' Morris on drums, John Olver on lead guitar, Jon Hall on vocals and yours truly on keyboards. The curtains drew back and with a cry of 'Good evening, all' we struck up a distinctly poor imitation of the Blues Brothers. This lasted approximately four bars before we noticed an extremely irate Geoff Cooke standing on the dance floor, none too impressed by what he heard or saw. I looked around and saw, to my horror, that the wiser, senior members of the band had quietly melted into the night, leaving me to – sorry – face the music. As I staggered back to my room, tail between my legs, I bumped into Nigel Redman. He commented that he saw Geoff in a different light – he usually showed great form after being up with the lads at three in the morning. I can assure you that the hour-long basting some six hours later soon changed his mind.

But enough of nostalgia and on to my ten commandments of touring. These should not be taken as gospel truths but merely as an aid to the well-being of the tour party.

The first and undoubtedly the most important commandment on any tour is: *Thou shalt not take thyself too seriously.* It has been well documented throughout the ages that rugby players have an inimitable sense of humour, which tends to prey on the short-comings of their colleagues. On tour the herd mentality is rife, and God help you if you find yourself in the firing line. Once the merest chink in your armour is exposed then the whole team will descend upon you like a ton of bricks. The best form of defence, both on and off the pitch, is attack. If you find yourself up against the proverbial ropes, just start swinging – verbally or otherwise. Fortu-nately, with so much going on on tour, there will always be another story to divert the herd's attention. A small tip is to be discreet, and if you're found out, don't fret. Another 'night after' story will soon emerge and your slow dance with the septuagenarian widow will soon be forgotten.

The second commandment is: *Thou shalt honour 'Drives'.* A common oversight on most tours is the need to keep the support team happy. There can be nothing more damaging than upsetting the driver of the tour bus. He should be humoured at all times and the bus should be treated with utmost respect. It is inadvisable to follow the actions of the members of a certain London medical-school rugby club, who removed a urinal from the opposition dress-ing rooms, put it on the back seat of the bus and used it *sans* plumbing. This is, after all, the man who controls your immediate destiny – be it on the M40 when you're dying to relieve your bladder or when you're trying to sneak a few beers on board for the homeward journey after an away game. Look after 'Drives' and he'll return the compliment. Cross him, and then see how you're left when he abandons you on the hard shoulder of the M3 on a wet Saturday night . . .

Third: *Thou shalt keep the Sabbath holy.* One of the many joys of touring is the God-given right not to play on a Sunday. Be it strong religious beliefs or simply a bastard behind the eyes, use this commandment wisely and maintain a sense of moral perspective on the game.

Number four: *Thou shalt obey the manager at all times.* A vital element in the tour party is the manager. Usually a 'forces man', he wears his blazer with pride and is always happy to recall the good old days of capital punishment. Known affectionately to the troops as 'Rear Gunner', he tries to run the tour with military precision, and invariably fails. It is important, however, to keep in with him for it is he who allocates the billets and the beer kitty, and makes the all-important decisions as to dress code. He always packs his boots (white laces compulsory) 'just in case' and can be found at the end of the night slumped in a corner, singing medleys. Lest we forget.

Numbers five, six and seven: *Thou shalt not kill/commit adultery/ covet thy billet's wife/daughter.* If adhered to strictly these commandments tend to help tour morale considerably.

Number eight: *Thou shalt not steal.* While all tourists are encouraged to return from the trip with a memento or two, the infamous Willie Anderson incident should serve as a sharp reminder of what may happen if you get caught. The former Irish captain was detained in Argentina following a run-in with the local constabulary about a missing national flag. Three months later he was finally released to tell his tale and become a shining example to each and every tourist of what may happen if you're caught. Beware: Big Brother may well be watching you.

Number nine: *Thou shalt not bear false witness against thy neighbour.* This can be roughly translated as 'Thou shalt not drop thy fellow tourist in it' if caught misbehaving on tour. If called to the Kangaroo Court and charged with heinous crimes, you should shoulder the blame yourself and not take anyone else down with you. Of course, this depends on whether they deserve it. An ancient tour maxim comes to mind: 'Don't shit on your mates unless you *really* have to.'

Finally, number ten: *Thou shalt not take the captain's name in vain.* Well . . . not within earshot, anyway.

I have had the privilege of travelling to five continents playing rugby and have many memories to enjoy, be they of bungee-jumping in Cairns or the thrill of meeting President Mandela at the historic first Test between South Africa and England in the summer of 1994 in Pretoria – and these are just off the pitch! My abiding memory of all the tours is undoubtedly the people I have met, both on and off the pitch. They are the rugby frontiersmen and -women who give so much to the game and who derive so much pleasure from spreading their gospel of rugby across the globe.

So my humble advice to anyone who may not have been fortunate enough to go on a rugby tour is: if you get a sniff of a chance, pack your boots, grab your passport and go. Touring has become an inherent part of my life. It is an addiction I hope I will never kick.

On Captaincy

DAVID HANDS

One of the sadder decisions taken by the International Rugby Football Board in recent years – and there have been some of remarkable sadness – was that which permitted the coach to take the field at half-time in representative games to instruct his team. So what? you may say. It's the coach who is responsible for the team preparation, and why should he not continue the process half-way through a match?

I will tell you why not. The decision marks the continued erosion of the ability of players to think for themselves, to make decisions on the hoof, to recognize, in a game of considerable chance, when to pull the strings. It is a process, in the northern hemisphere at any rate, that stems from the recognition in the 1960s that coaching was a virtue yet, taken to extremes, could turn players into automatons, blindly following the 'game plan' and bereft of recognition of the opportunities which, in a game involving thirty players, could arise at any time.

Not that England, with France the leaders of the game in the north over the last decade, have generally distinguished themselves in the matter of leadership but it does not augur well that the position of captain should be further undermined. There were some poignant scenes involving France, before their resurgence in 1993 and 1994, when their half-backs clearly looked for guidance to the stands where sat their authoritarian coach, Pierre Berbizier; there could be no surer sign of a team lacking individual or cohesive confidence and the prospects of success must have been slim.

Significantly, Kitch Christie, coach to South Africa in 1994 and 1995, opposed the move to allow coaches on the pitch – perhaps because his contribution to rugby in his country is only part of his existence. As a successful businessman he was in a position to take or leave the national position when it was offered him and he therefore recognizes that others must be given the opportunity to succeed or fail, in sport as well as in life itself.

Perhaps in that sense the crisis in leadership in sport – if that is not too strong a phrase – reflects merely the time in which we live. Every area of public life is under intense scrutiny: institutions and individuals can be so easily portrayed as failures if they do not match up to an exacting and frequently artificial standard imposed by those, within the media and outside, who do not have to deal directly in authority. Unfortunately the critics do not always make a proper distinction between different jobs, but assume that if a failing is discovered in one area, that must necessarily impinge on all others.

There is a danger that this could become a social rather than sporting monologue but I have no doubt that there comes a time when players must be left to their own devices, when the coach must relinquish responsibility into the hands of his chosen representatives – the fifteen players on the park and their nominated leaders, the captain, pack leader and director of the backs (although, of course, two of those roles may be contained in the same individual). That is part of the magic of sport: that for all the preparation, the hours in video-study, the technical analysis of the opposition, on the day the verdict can hang on the contrary bounce of a ball and one man's ability to seize opportunity before it hurries by.

What, after all, do we want sport to be? Should it be the domain of coaches, forever trying to produce the perfect game in an imperfect world, or should it reflect the (usually) youthful ebullience and occasional naïveté of the players? Surely, at its best, sport is the conflict of individuals or teams during which each strives for mastery over a given time, both performers and spectators recognizing the patterns that unfold before them in the knowledge that those picked for the role were perceived to be the best of their kind and also bear the responsibility for the quality of their display. Every player on the team carries responsibility, but the captain more than any and, once the gladiators take to the arena, the coach's part in the proceedings is over.

Good captains, it is said, are born not made, which may bear out the belief of coarse rugby players: that the captain is the son either of the chairman of selectors or of the woman who washes the team kit every Saturday night. Wavell Wakefield, one of the acknowledged great players of English rugby, said: 'There is usually in every school or club a player of outstanding personality who is clearly fitted to lead the team. To such a man, whether he be the best player or not, the captaincy must go.' English cricket offers an outstanding example of this in Mike Brearley, who was seldom the popular choice as opening batsman but whose pure cricketing ability was bolstered by his leadership qualities.

Wakefield, of course, led an outstanding team during the 1920s and it is arguable that no captain will earn his place in sport's hall of fame without being part of a side including several players of great quality. Particularly is this true of rugby: if the ideal number for a committee is one, then the greater the number of players on the field, the greater the capacity for error. In a physical-contact game such as rugby union, the potential for error is magnified still further. It is probably the most difficult international team sport in which to succeed, and it is no surprise that the roll-call of good captains heavily favours the nation which has made the closest study of the game and its tactics – New Zealand. Even for those of us who live on the other side of the world, it takes no great effort to remember outstanding All Black captains: Wilson Whineray, Brian Lochore, Graham Mourie, David Kirk, Wayne Shelford – and those from only a thirty-year, post-war period. Try the same exercise for British and Irish rugby and see how many names can match that quintet for tried and tested quality; we are talking here of players whose recognition of strategy and tactics has shaped significant matches.

New Zealanders know the nuts and bolts of the game: they have grown up with it, lived and loved it, studied it from an early age, and when they assume positions of responsibility – and that does not necessarily mean team captaincy but leadership of the pack or calling the backs' moves – they are comfortable with it. Not only that, they know they are surrounded by fourteen others who, by and large, think the same way. Even in New Zealand there is the occasional maverick, such as the delightfully un-All Black stand-off-half, Bob Burgess (he of the flowing locks and liberal moustache in the early 1970s), but it makes the role of captain vastly easier if every player is tuned to the same wavelength.

Those fine players and wordsmiths of an early age, Dave Gallaher and Billy Stead, captain and vice-captain respectively of the 1905 New Zealand touring team in Britain, laid down demanding criteria for their ideal captain, criteria which I suspect have only recently been recognized in their totality in Britain. He must, they agreed, know all there is to be known about the theory and practice of the game, be possessed of acute perception and knowledge of human nature, be armed with the strengths and weaknesses not only of his own men but, so far as possible, those of the opposition. But one of his first duties, Gallaher and Stead suggest, 'is to see that all his men are in general agreement on main points'.

The 1991 World Cup in Britain provided two remarkable illustrations of this: one in the opening match of the tournament, the other in the closing match. Both involved England, at Twickenham. On the opening day, New Zealand were captained by Gary Whetton, one of their finest lock-forwards but a short-term captain who found himself involved in a game of nip and tuck as both sides shadow-boxed and Jonathan Webb exchanged penalty goals with Grant Fox. A dropped goal by Rob Andrew gave England a tenuous 12–9 lead, which is when Whetton and his chief lieutenant, Fox, visibly wound up the elastic and increased the pace of the game.

Admittedly, Whetton possessed in his XV a player ideally suited to do so in Michael Jones, the Auckland flanker. It was he who scored the game-breaking try but it takes more than one player to lift the tempo of a match to such a degree that England forwards who played in it admitted they suddenly found themselves left trailing. In New Zealand eyes, nothing subtle occurred, merely the recognition of the overall situation and what was required to break the pattern – it was enough.

Compare and contrast this with the final, four weeks later, played between England and Australia. Whatever may have been said much later, in the immediate aftermath of Australia's 12–6 win, both the England coach and the England forwards were furious at the departure from the tight-knit, forward-based plan that had taken England so far. It was a classic case of the England backs becoming so possessed of a strategy with which they had insufficient familiarity that they ran the ball over-zealously, out of reach of their powerful mauling pack. One half of the side was out of step with what the other half was doing and, whatever is said to the contrary, I cannot believe that this was a concerted team decision taken before the final. Even if it was, recognition of requirements on the day was absent: early in the match Marty Roebuck, the Australian full-back, was hit heavily in a tackle under a high ball and required attention. If memory serves he did not receive a similar test at any stage thereafter, for which he must have been profoundly grateful.

England's captain on that occasion was Will Carling, who has led an international side more frequently than any one else in the world. Carling is an instructive study: he is a captain very much in the modern mould, who follows – inadvertently or not – many of the requirements laid down by Gallaher and Stead. His is state-of-the-art captaincy, hinged on personal contact with team members, sympathetic treatment of individuals, and keen study of opponents. Thrown into the job at the age of twenty-two, Carling was forced to learn on the hoof but all the application in the world does not create a natural tactician: when the chips are down, steady adherence to the game plan – a naturally English trait – may not necessarily win the match.

The situation that always returns to haunt Carling is the Grand

Slam match of 1990 between Scotland and England, in which England began as overwhelming favourites – and lost. At certain times during that game, decisions had to be made, crucial to the outcome, and from the sidelines it was not evident that Carling was completely in command. In his authorized biography Carling later admitted: 'At the end of the day, I'm the captain. And I'm the one who's going to live or die by those decisions. Although I would still ask and listen, I have to decide the way it's going to be. At Murrayfield I didn't assert myself enough.' It was a frank admission that captaincy by committee, in the emotional turmoil of an international occasion, will not work and an important step on Carling's road towards maturity as a leader.

He has had Murrayfield 1990 thrown in his face so frequently that the sidestep has long been worked out but there are other examples: would England have won a Grand Slam in 1991 but for a slice of unpremeditated individual genius by Rory Underwood against Ireland? How did the games against Wales in Cardiff in 1989 and, more particularly, 1993 get away from the side that seemed so plainly superior?

Experience, as well as knowledge of the game, must play a part. When Bill Beaumont was first appointed to lead England in 1978 he was a far from logical choice but by dint of perseverance and that quality of leading from the front which so appeals to the English, he turned himself into a captain of quality. To begin with Beaumont was fortunate in his aides: his pack was littered with former captains in Fran Cotton, Tony Neary and Roger Uttley, all of them with a reservoir of experience and knowledge on which he could draw. But as time went on he learned his trade – so well, in fact, that he led England to their 1980 Grand Slam and captained the British Lions on the back of it. More than likely he would have led the 1983 Lions, too, but for the head injury which forced his premature retirement from the game.

But the criteria for captaincy in the rugby world of the 1990s have changed immeasurably since Beaumont's day, most notably in public duties. It was always the captain's lot to stand up and say the right things in public, usually at the post-match dinner. But now they are required by the demands of a voracious media to be instant analysts, instantly available, their merest shake of a resigned head subject to criticism. Nowhere in English team sports has this demand been more obviously apparent than in cricket, where one could only feel for Michael Atherton as he tried yet again, during some deeply depressing days in 1994, to defend the indefensible performances of his colleagues.

Rugby has joined the ranks of high-profile world sports and, in doing so, has descended into cliché because there are only so many different answers which can be given to the same questions. Yet here again, the New Zealand experience serves as well as any because of their depth of knowledge of the game: thus David Kirk, asked after the 1987 World Cup final against France whether it might not have been better to have offered a more entertaining game, replied: 'You blokes make me laugh. That was a Test match.'

Yet trial by media is no laughing matter. Players have become spokesmen for the game, a responsibility that some handle far better than others, and the captain is required always to be the perfect ambassador, even when his team has just lost in the most draining of circumstances. The tears shed by Gavin Hastings, in the immediate aftermath of Scotland's one-point defeat by England in 1994, betrayed to the television camera, more poignantly than anything, the unreasonable demands to be made of a captain.

The Australians, recognizing before many other countries the need for their sportsmen to bolster the image of their game, have introduced courses for their players both in rugby and cricket in how to handle contact with the media. They have, though, been blessed with leaders who have handled that aspect well without specific training. There is no better example of a player who could cope with everything that came his way, on and off the field, than Nick Farr-Jones, the scrum-half who must surely have learned some of the public arts from his first coach, the voluble and sometimes brilliant Alan Jones. There was never a moment when Jones, on tour in Britain in 1984, would not or could not go head to head with the media; for a young man on his first Wallabies tour, it was a potent example of the dos and don'ts in the performing art of the public front.

When justifying the decision to make Farr-Jones captain, Bob Dwyer (Australia's coach) said: 'Nick is a great student of the game and he is respected by all his peers.' Which, broadly speaking, takes us back to Gallaher and Stead and their demand that no captain should be at a loss on either the game's laws or the strengths and weaknesses of his playing colleagues.

But the game has changed out of all recognition since the first All Blacks careered their way round the four home countries just after the turn of the century. Quite apart from law changes designed to 'improve' rugby, it has become harder, faster, stronger: if one side gets the whip hand over the other nowadays, the game can gallop away in a welter of seven-point scores so that a team starting indifferently may find themselves looking at a thirty-point deficit even before they reach the interval (look at England in the World Cup semi-final against New Zealand!). That then becomes a burdensome hill to climb. In more static days, a team might play poorly but defend just well enough to keep their opposition to a couple of three-point tries and a penalty: 9–0 seems far more surmountable than 30–0.

That is another aspect of captaincy which has become even more demanding than Gallaher and Stead recognized: 'Personally we remember some astonishing cases of sides being many points down a few minutes from the end, and winning easily by the aid of nothing else but [this] sudden change of tactics on the part of the captain,' the two New Zealanders wrote. That might have been so but is rarely the case in representative rugby at our end of the twentieth century, where to play the waiting game they advocate may be the precursor of disaster.

And always haunting rugby in Britain has been, until late in the century, its *ad hoc* nature. Those who play the game now at representative level, with their constant squad meetings, their three days together before internationals, may not easily identify with the habits of their predecessors, who would turn up the day before an international, meet their colleagues – sometimes for the first time – run through a few back movements and play twenty-four hours later. British rugby in general, English rugby in particular, has made spectacular changes in custom and attitude over the last decade and that, in turn, has impinged directly on the captain.

Certain principles remain, including the recommended position for a captain to occupy. It is one of those historical curiosities that hookers have frequently turned up as international captains, for all that every pundit believes that a player with his head buried in the scrum cannot make accurate assessments of the drift of a match. The counterweight to that is that a hooker, at the core of his team, may 'feel' quite perceptibly the rising and falling strength of his team and also that anyone who plays at the coal face is more than likely to possess the character required to lead a side.

In general, though, the middle five – back row and half-back – are the most appropriate positions for a captain, because not only can he have a reasonable appreciation of the trend of a game but he is in a position directly to do something about it and to remain in contact with both backs and forwards. Back row has been described as the 'thinking man's position' (mostly by back-row forwards) and knowledge of the law, and how to circumvent it, is legendary among flank forwards: of modern players, South Africa's Pienaar and Shelford, the New Zealand and latterly Northampton number eight, fall into this category, and there are numerous others at lesser levels, many of whom go on to become coaches of distinction.

Half-back has often been criticized as an ideal area of captaincy because it is deemed to place undue responsibility on the shoulders of players who are, by the nature of their positions, the pivots of the side. Against that is the ability of such players at once to accept both playing and, by inference, tactical responsibilities. Of these, Farr-Jones and Kirk are prime examples, while in France, down the years, the scrum-half has captained many a representative team even though, of late, they have gone from a hooker to lock to in fairly short order. In the case of Philippe Saint-André, the Montferrand wing who was given the leadership late in the 1993–4 season, personality was also a significant factor: Saint-André is not only a talented player but a bubbling, cheerful soul who commands affection as well as respect.

Indeed, one single act has probably implanted Saint-André in rugby's history books for all time: before the summer of 1994 he was remembered as the player who scored one of the great tries at Twickenham , in 1991, by being on the end of the move which swept from south to north, but which was inspired by Blanco and Berbizier and owed almost everything thereafter to the speed of Philippe Sella and the vision and technical excellence of Didier Camberabero. After 1994, however, Saint-André is remembered as the man who inspired what he later described as 'the try from the end of the world'.

'Courage,' as W. J. A. Davies, that great England stand-off-half and captain of the 1920s, remarked, 'is required in a marked degree from a captain. He should strive to go all out for a win, and to take sufficient risks to ensure this. Many captains fear their fate overmuch, and are rarely bold enough; but the spirit of rugby football is to play as daringly as the circumstances admit, and every captain should endeavour to stimulate his side to take risks, instead of playing for safety.' Davies would have approved of Saint-André's decision to run ball from his own 22 against the All Blacks and thus provoke not only a match-winning try but a series win – the first by France in New Zealand.

That score was captured for all time on television, the medium that has had a dramatic impact on sport, in the general and particular sense. The camera portrays sport with warts and all, and has contributed hugely to the cleansing of an image which, previously, could get away with much, either because it went unseen by the majority or because those who reported it accepted rugby as a game in which if you could not stand the heat you removed yourself from the kitchen. I have always believed that the pack led by Wakefield, for all its playing record during the 1920s, was probably one of the rougher, tougher assortments ever purveyed by England, which might have contributed substantially to the incident in which Cyril Brownlie became the first player ever to be sent off in an international, playing for New Zealand at Twickenham in 1925. What, I wonder, would the slow-motion replay have made of that?

The camera, too, has power to emphasize in a way that thousands of words never can. Sometimes to over-emphasize. The replay of violent incidents can create a misleading impression of the game as a whole, and this all falls now within the captain's remit. He must not only demonstrate before a host of critics, many of whom have themselves played international rugby and led international teams, that he has a thorough grasp of affairs on the field, but he must have the public-relations ability to justify or explain the game off the field.

We are seeking paragons who cannot, will not, exist. That rugby has captains of distinction, whose public image enhances the game and whose willingness to work hard on rugby's behalf is clear, is rugby's good fortune. The new-age rugby leaders – like Will Carling and François Pienaar, Ieuan Evans in Wales and Michael Lynagh in Australia – have shown themselves to be outstanding communicators who understand their sporting milieu sufficiently well to know that they can enhance not only their game but their own career prospects. Who would blame them for that?

Bath – From a Rear-View Mirror
The Eve of the Cup Final

STUART BARNES

Bloody hell; I hate this damned Bath traffic. I know this place is famous as a spa town, a leisurely city, but surely not everyone leaves work at 3.00 p.m. on a Friday afternoon? Four o'clock – I don't know why the office insist on me arriving here now. Half the players will saunter along at half past the hour. I hope they're in more of a hurry tomorrow or those Leicester boys will shock them. That would teach some of those cocky sods a lesson. Mind you, it will be a pretty miserable journey back down the M4 from London tomorrow night.

It will probably take until kick-off to escape from this traffic. I could have picked up the kids from school and earned some Brownie points with the missus. Instead I'm sat here in this bloody awful blazer, waiting for Nigel Redman. Like waiting for Godot.

He's always last. I'm surprised he shows his face sometimes – he's handed so much abuse by that lot. Last away league game he lumbered on to the bus so late that I think Richard Hill was already £25 down in that eternal bloody three-card-brag school they have. I like Nigel Redman. He's more polite than most of them, but when some of those roaring boys, veins popping in their foreheads, started shouting at him, ''Ere, Ollie [don't ask me why he's called Ollie, probably from Laurel and Hardy], how come you're always last on the bus?' and he replied in that slow and thoughtful way that gives him a stupid appearance until you get to know him, 'I hate being kept waiting, so I make sure I am the last bloke on the bus,' well, that card-school set exploded like the Fifth of November. Not much can distract those little half-backs, Hill and Barnes, from the card table, but even they forgot the draw for a full minute to concentrate on throwing some verbal acid at him. He deserved it, but *I* wouldn't stand for the abuse they give him. It's worse for him but those boys are happy to turn at the drop of a hat (or card) and lash out at someone else. Everyone is abused. I suppose that the only time they might really worry is if nobody's shouting at them. That normally means the rest are talking behind their back. Talk about women, this lot gossip better than they play rugby.

Bad-mouthing, swearing, taking the piss out of each other all the time – God knows how they keep winning when they seem to hate each other so much. Strangest group I've ever driven. It's fine if they all gang up on Graham Dawe, for example, but if a Harlequin or Bristol player even suggested he was not one of the greatest men since Jesus, Dawesy would be defended by all of them.

Anyway, what *is* the time? Five to four. Here's John Allen, the first-team secretary, and old Ken with the kit. Don't ask me what John derives from this. He doesn't get paid. All he receives is a load more abuse from those baboons at the back of the bus. Why doesn't he tell them to sort themselves out? Half of them couldn't even find their way to an away match. It's great being able to bluff a hand on a king high but it wouldn't help them find their way to Wasps.

The only time some of them speak to John is to blame him for something. If a hint of politeness enters their voices you know they want some coffee from the machine on the bus. Thank God it's so bloody weak. They drink so much of it that they'd probably fail a drugs test on caffeine levels if there were any.

Ah, here comes the physiotherapist, Julie Bardner. She's a decent, civilized lady. That doesn't stop them taking the piss out of her. She ignores them; probably can't be bothered with them. She reads books that aren't by Barbara Cartland or that bloke who's always in the courts – whatsisname ... Jeffrey Archer. The only time

Barnesy's civilized is when he asks her what she's reading. He's supposed to be a bit of a literary type but I've never seen him read anything except ace, king, queen and jack on the coach. He won't be late. He likes to be early to guarantee his regular seat at the card table. Richard Hill sits next to him. When I look in my mirror I can see a load of grey on one head and a shiny little bald patch on the other. Back of Hill's head is a bit like a cricket wicket. Lots of grass at the start, but going bare by the end of a Test match. I bet that Shane Warne could spin a cricket ball off Hilly!

He might be losing his hair, but he's always respectable. Properly dressed like rugby players should be. Most of them look more like a pop group. That's what Jack always calls them. Thank God they haven't made a single – there are some bloody awful voices in that team. Of course, they won't be singing on the way to the match – they might lose their concentration on those cards. I can't get used to the changes in personnel around the table this season. Old Coochie's retired and nobody has claimed his seat opposite Barnesy. Whoever sits there won't give him that glare that Chilcott used to. Most normal people would rush into the toilet when they saw that 'I'm going to win this hand' look. Guscott's been missing as well. All the papers write about Bath and England missing his play; most of this bunch probably miss his cards more. Not as loud as Chilcott but he has a tongue on him. He says some shocking things and then laughs his head off like a hyena, as if to say 'only joking'. I wouldn't suffer that sort of behaviour but the boys certainly like him.

Look who's arrived. Barnes and Swift. What a pair. One's a gambler and the other sits at the front reading his Harvard Business School books. Bloody business gurus. Swifty reckons England dropped him once because he looked worried – and miserable, I'd add. He doesn't look as if he's enjoying himself but he's always an early arriver in his shell suit. I expect it's an escape for an accountant to leave his office and just listen to the rest of those silly bastards in the team.

I suppose I should offer to help start loading the gear, 'Afternoon,

John, Tony, Stuart. 'Ere, Barnesy, how much can we expect you to lose today?' He's just told me to 'shut up and load this coach, you old bastard'. I was only making conversation. Nothing wrong with small talk. I hope the little shit loses every penny he's brought.

Most of the boys are now arriving, but there's still no sign of Redman and Robinson. Robbo's absence will annoy the card school. He's a regular. Who's playing today, anyway? I can see those poison dwarves Hill and Barnes . . . Catt's there, de Glanville – he suffers tons of abuse, too. He always has a go back but they shout him down; especially that big old bugger Ojomoh. Calls him 'blouse'.

Callard's playing as well. He hates it when they call him Zanussi. They claim his head is the shape of a microwave. They all babble a childish Japanese. Most of them make no sense in English. They think I'm a dull old 'drives' but even I could tell them Zanussi is Italian. Callard loses enough money to remind me of the Italian economy. At least he's honest, not like some of those foreigners – not that I've got anything against them, mind.

Ojomoh doesn't play cards; I don't think he has the energy. All of them extract the Michael from the Nigerians, but they don't really think them any different from anyone else. If you play for Bath they wouldn't care if you were an ex-convict as long as you played well. 'Hello, Robbo.' There he goes, straight into his wallet. Just Redman now.

Half past four. What did I say? Ah, here he is at last. 'All on.' They're at it again, just shouted, 'Shut up and drive.' I've got bloody feelings. I wish they'd remember that. I'll just indicate right and we're off. Bloody hell, there are hundreds of people decked out in their Bath colours. If only they knew what sort of bunch they idolize – hero-worship – it's bloody stupid.

Thousands of them will be travelling to Twickenham tomorrow. This team might be a bad bunch but they keep us drivers in business with these Cup finals. Either way the bars will do a roaring trade. Punters explaining what will happen tonight, and what happened tomorrow. Wouldn't be so keen if they knew them. Mind you, they are polite to supporters, they do wave back and most of them even talk to them after a match. Obviously not as big stars as some fans think they are. I just wish they didn't have to be so rude on the coach.

First stop, and I'm just ten minutes from the ground. We always have to hire two videos. One is always violent and usually chosen by the Nigerians. I reckon they see themselves as the Bath equivalent of a Los Angeles ghetto gang. Don't ask me how Adedayo Adebayo can kid himself; according to the boys, he has more money than all of them put together. Now why is Jon Hall diving into the toilet? Ah, apparently he owes the shop some money for a video he hasn't returned. Listen to them . . . laughing at their captain like a disrespectful bunch of hyenas. 'No, missus, he's not on the coach, honestly.' I bloody hate having to lie for them. 'Hally, that's the last time I lie for you.' What a surprise. I've been told to shut up again. Ungrateful so-and-so.

On the motorway now. They'll settle down into their video until the first machine-gun cross-fire action scene lays waste to an entire town, leaving seventy-two people dead in the process. Then Barnes will holler, 'Turn that fucking video down,' and everyone watching will tell him to piss off without taking their eyes from the screen. The television generation. Television or card addicts, none of them have any manners.

Jon Hall's walking to the front, accompanied by those hysterical hyena yelps. He's been fleeced. So much for team spirit.

The card school look more nervous about the next deal than tomorrow's final with Leicester. Me, I'm not that keen on rugby, but I've never missed a final. You know, always been working so if I get a ticket, might as well watch the game.

I won't forget when we – er, *they* – beat the Wasps. Old Halliday scored near the end and I sprinted on to that pitch. Robbie Lye was next to me. I said, 'Blimey, Robbie, how come you're invading the pitch? You played twenty years for this team.' He just laughed and hugged me. Something then flew into my eye.

At last, the exit for Runnymede. Those buggers losing at cards will be furious that I've driven so fast. They won't have time to claw back their money. Let's just hope that Barnes is losing.

Hah! Good news, Barnes *and* Hill lost; that will mean that it won't be quite so noisy at dinner – apart from de Glanville going on and on. I'll just park the bus and let them all scramble for their room keys. I'd hate to be the poor hotel receptionist who has to try and deal with that lot. Mind you, the players won't get their rooms first. They might be young and fit but they don't have the experience of the committee men who have travelled on the bus. It will be they who obtain the keys, they who are first to dinner and they who keep the club's tab running at the bar until three in the morning. They reckon the club couldn't run without them, but I wonder how Bath would perform if fifteen committee men took the field tomorrow? When half of them were playing, a win against Weston-super-Mare on tour was a reason for celebration.

Well, there goes the last of them. I'll just get my key and head down for dinner. If I can find a table anywhere near the players I might be able to scrounge a glass of something decent. I'll be buggered if any of them know more about wine than how to open their mouths and pour it down, but they know plenty about spending other people's money. If there's a wine at £50 and one at £25 they'll order the expensive one. I don't blame them. Every time the committee cock up the finances of the club they mutter about players' expenses, away trips and all that. Fair enough if they did nothing for the club, but this lot have won cup after cup and four leagues running. I reckon it's they, and not the committee, who should take credit for the new members and the sponsorship. Imagine if SWEB had sponsored the club because of the committee: 'Come and see twenty-seven or so old blokes, most of them with nothing better to do, muck up England's best team if you give them half a chance.'

It might be a Cup final tomorrow but not many of them seem interested in pasta or chicken – I thought that was what athletes were supposed to eat before a big match. Roast beef, venison curry, a bit of fish: that's fair enough . . . but with all that wine and the puddings, I don't know how they're allowed to do it. But there's nobody to stop them, is there? The blokes are amateurs, they can eat whatever they want, do whatever they want. They know that if they lose they will be abused in all the national papers and the rest of England will celebrate, so they must be confident that they aren't being too excessive. None of them will stay late. They'll all be in bed by midnight. Most of them watch that programme *The Word* or an in-house movie, but old Swifty is probably reading John Harvey-Jones. Odd lot, really. Bedtime for me.

Saturday, early morning. I love breakfasts in these hotels. A lovely big greasy plateful and no wife to say, 'I cooked it, you clear it up.' No wonder the players like staying away on a Friday night. Some of them beat me down to breakfast this morning. I used to think it was nerves but now I realize it's the ones who are used to getting up early. Graham Dawe is the exception. He rises so bloody early as a farmer that he enjoys a sleep in. Swift is one of them, so's Barnesy. Richard Hill won't be far behind. Chilcott used to be one of the late ones, but now it's Jon Hall. He must disappear to bed at 9.00 p.m. as well on a Friday night. No wonder they call him 'half man half bed'.

It doesn't matter whether they come early or late to breakfast, one thing they nearly all do is read the newspaper previews. Most of them swear and cuss, but they're like moths around a candle. They love it if one of them is abused by several papers – that raises a smile. Of course, the worst of them all is Jack Rowell. Swears that he never reads a paper but he seems to be aware of every word that every reporter has written about him or his team. If he is really angry about an article he will say, 'My wife says that in the . . .' I can only assume that Sue Rowell takes a sadistic pleasure in reading about disastrous matches.

After breakfast Nigel Redman will take his regular stroll along the Thames; Dawesy will have another haircut and the others will sit around abusing each other. You wouldn't guess that it's one of the biggest days of the season; not until they disappear into a room for their team meeting. Whatever is said in that room, they all emerge as different people.

The loud ones who take the piss out of the quieter younger ones are now whispering in the ears of the blokes they were embarrassing before they walked into the room. Just like lovers, arguing one minute and intimate the next. All the wisecracking has disappeared. The only real noise comes from those big old forwards. Graham Dawe looks more intimidating than anything I've ever seen in a horror movie. 'Come on,' he bellows, except it sounds like incitement to violence. I saw the film *Silence of the Lambs*. Some of those forwards' eyes remind me of Anthony Hopkins's. If the teams this lot play are also amateurs I reckon they're all stark, staring mad. I wouldn't do it for all the tea in China . . . course I wouldn't – I don't even like tea. All right, then, for all the beer in all the barrels . . . Well, perhaps I'd risk it.

Dawe is one of the most frightening of them. You can see his muscles tense beneath his shirt. He's got the biggest hands I've ever seen. Even his fingers look knotted with muscles. I don't know what it is about sport but something snaps in the brain when it stops being playtime. Dawe's been travelling up and down the M5 from Launceston for over ten years now. I can imagine him driving – thinking about nothing but making life hell for his opposite hooker. Playing against him must be like rubbing your cheek on sandpaper for eighty minutes. No, thank you.

I can't even hear any abuse from the back of the coach. That's probably because they never have a card school on the way to the match. Jon Hall sits with his back to me – so wide he covers half the bus. Barnes hardly raises his head. He prepares himself for the game on the bus. He won't notice, and he certainly won't acknowledge, anybody before the match. All of them have been here so often but this five-mile journey is always the same. How I envy all the other coach drivers. Busloads of boisterous Bath fans. OK, I'd not want to clean up all the cider they spill, but it's good-humoured excitement – a day out. There's no pleasure here, just a tension so tight you almost feel yourself being strangled. Only Victor's voice punctures the silence. He's got a laugh that can annoy you but, on this journey, it sounds like a waterfall in the desert.

Big Jack's alongside me, looking straight ahead. I've never seen a less convincing smile in my life. Christ, let me get them off this bus.

'I've got the team on the bus, mate. Here's my pass for the West Car Park.' Not many supporters who park here on an international day would bother talking to the likes of me . . . I don't own a BMW. It's different today, though. No stupid patriots supporting fifteen blokes they don't know and probably wouldn't like if they did. On a Cup final day, all the Bath boys seem to know the thousands in blue, black and white. There's the players' wives, probably been drinking all morning. How often have I heard the players moan, 'I'd rather be in the car park'? But they wouldn't. Having driven this lot to all those matches, I reckon I could tell a few people a thing or two about what it takes to win. As they get off the bus, heads up, slow walk, I get the feeling that they're rehearsing walking through a brick wall that stands between them and another trophy. 'Come on, let's kill them.' That's Graham Dawe leaving his seat. A few of them just touch each other – a gentle hand on the back, or the shoulder. They've been through so much together they hardly need to speak. They know what those little gestures mean.

They're gone now. Hill and Barnes have disappeared straight away but I can still see Ben Clarke and Andy Reed's head. If I could see the bald head of Nigel Redman he might still be in the England team . . .

'Go on Catty, yeeeesssss! That's it! No way Leicester can come back now. Look at Mike punching the air . . . Yeahh! Come on, Bath.'

The old bastards have done it again. Full circle. No discipline, half of them were late arriving for the bus yesterday; no manners – they're the rudest sods I've ever heard; not even much healthy eating . . . red wine and pudding. But, bugger me, I knew when I saw them come out of Rowell's team meeting that they'd win. Some of the players claim they know before kick-off, from the behaviour of their mates, how the match will go. When you spend time with them, you know what they mean. Mind you, I've got the worst journey of all the Bath coach drivers now. Most of the others will find half their passengers are asleep: pissed, exhausted or both. This lot are going to be flying on adrenaline all night.

The bus is due to leave the car park at six. It's ten past and only four of them are on it. Still, I forgive them today; I'll be the most envied driver on the motorway. They won't be long because Twickenham closes the bar in the old tea-room where they stuff the players after a final. A couple of sandwiches, two sausage rolls and a watery pint of beer . . . it doesn't matter how many wives and relatives are in the room, they'll be here shortly. I've got the four cases of beer on the bus. They always want more than they drink. I don't know why they drink a pint from a glass in five minutes and a can on the bus in thirty, but they do and they never learn the lesson.

Ah, here they come. Jack Rowell's glasses are in his top pocket. He must be expecting a few people to take pictures of him tonight. The rest of them are straggling out . . . Just Ollie left. 'Come on, Redman!' They're off again. This is going to be a long journey. 'Lads, I'm due back by nine, OK?' 'No problem,' says Jon Hall. 'We're just going to stop for one at the Pheasant.' That's a pub just off the A338 near Wantage. The boys have been drinking there for years now. The owner knows them like they're locals . . . in fact, I think some of them almost are. Barnes, Clarke, Rowell, Hill, Guscott . . . they'll all be on the real ale – 6X, I think. Chilcott will have the younger forwards on the Guinness while a few will drink lager. Sanders, Ojo.

They all want a pint but about ten of them have got to have a piss first . . . I love those subtle gear changes. 'Only half an hour, lads.' I don't know why I bother. They'll have at least four pints. They'll probably try and lace some of the beer snobs' drinks with vodka to see if they notice, and then they'll meander out and look all sheepish. 'Sorry we're late, couldn't get so and so out of the bar.' If they'd lost I wouldn't wait for them.

103

Swifty's giggling, forgotten all about accountancy, Rowell is call-ing everyone a 'bad man' and Guscott – what's he doing here? He didn't play – he's laughing at the opposition. Whatever else they are, they're not humble in victory. Guscott loves to imagine how they feel. Barnes and Swift have lost finals, but it's so long ago that they probably don't remember. Let's go.

Back in Bath. This is the worst part of the night. They're pissed so they don't moan as much as they usually would. I'll drop them off by the ground on Pulteney Street and pop in for a beer. The clubhouse is full of supporters. They get a great reception from the fans – they like that – but then they have a buffet reception in a cordoned-off part of the club. By the time they arrive, the commit-tee and their friends have left them a sausage roll each, the pineapple but not the cheese, and a few quiche crusts. No wonder they don't rate the committee.

They'll be out of the club before me, but they'll not sober up for two days. Tomorrow's a big party at Jack Rowell's house, an open-top bus ride and a civic reception. Good luck to the Mayor.

I wonder what it was like to have played in that team. I bet it was fun.

The bus driver in this story is purely fictitious and not based on the wonderful drivers who have driven Bath around the country for so many years. This mostly fictitious piece is dedicated to their tolerance and good humour.

John Rutherford and Attacking Back-Play

ALLAN MASSIE

For the last two years argument has raged in Scotland over the rival merits of Craig Chalmers and Gregor Townsend. It echoes, with a curious symmetry, the dispute that agitated English rugby over the previous ten years: should Rob Andrew or Stuart Barnes be England's fly-half? Supporters of Chalmers and Andrew point to their all-round competence, their reading of the game, the quality of their defensive kicking, and their willingness to tackle and take on defensive duties. Supporters of Townsend and Barnes argue (argued in the case of Barnes, since he has now, prematurely perhaps, retired) that the ability of Chalmers and Andrew to get the three-quarter line moving is questionable, and insist on their hero's ability to set the game alight with a scorching break.

Put crudely, competence of a high order is set against flair, although this is, of course, an over-simplification, Townsend and Barnes not being devoid of competence nor Andrew and Chalmers of flair. Nevertheless, it is an old argument repeated in many sports – Gooch v. Gower, for example.

In the 1995 Five Nations season, Andrew (with Barnes retired) and Chalmers came out on top. Moreover, Andrew, taking the ball flatter, was a more effective attacker, while Chalmers recovered the confidence and exuberance he lost after a series of injuries beginning with the Calcutta Cup match of 1993 – ironically, a match in which, Andrew having been dropped, Barnes gave his finest performance for England, while Townsend, coming on to replace Chalmers, had an unhappy time. In 1995 Scotland compromised by playing him, very effectively, at outside-centre.

Between 1979 and 1987, however, Scotland had a fly-half, John Rutherford, who, to a remarkable degree, combined the virtues of Chalmers and Townsend, Andrew and Barnes. That was the measure of his stature, authority and brilliance. In the middle eighties he was unquestionably the best fly-half in the northern hemisphere; and yet, such is the way fortune goes, he played only one Test for the British Lions – and that at inside-centre to Ollie Campbell, in the third Test against New Zealand on the un-happy 1983 tour. The game was played in atrocious conditions. He scored a try, but was injured and unable to play in the fourth Test. The inaugural World Cup in 1987 meant that the next Lions tour was not until 1989, by which time he had retired, and Chalmers (aged only twenty) and Andrew were the Lions' halves.

Rutherford's talent, even genius, was apparent from the first, but it was a long time before it was fully acknowledged outside Scotland, and even in Scotland there were at first some doubters. Yet Andy Irvine, the greatest Scottish player of the last quarter century, reckoned that 'of the stand-offs in my time Phil Bennett would be the only player of comparable class'.

John Rutherford was born in Selkirk on 4 October 1955, and went to the local high school, representing Scottish Schools in 1972. He played all his club rugby for Selkirk, and this had an important influence on the way he developed. Selkirk have almost always been one of the weaker clubs among the seven that make up the Border League. Rutherford was only the sixth international to come out of the club, which has only once won the Scottish championship, and that back in the days when it was unofficial. Unable to call on the resources of Hawick or Gala, or any of the big city clubs, Selkirk have rarely been able to field a big pack, so the backs have had to make do with short rations. This remained the case – although to a lesser extent – even after Rutherford had managed to attract Iain Paxton (who would subsequently go on the

1983 Lions tour with him) to the club. In his early years they even spent a season in the second division.

This being so, Rutherford, who captained the club for five seasons between 1977 and 1986, early learned to make the most of limited possession. Tall (by the standards of Welsh fly-halves), fast, beautifully built and a finely balanced runner, in his early days he was completely uninhibited. It took him some time to acquire the judgement he displayed at the peak of his career.

He came into the Scotland team when it was in the middle of a bad spell. The great pack of the late seventies, with a front five of McLauchlan, Madsen, Carmichael, Gordon Brown and Alastair McHarg, had broken up, and Scotland struggled, like Selkirk, to win enough ball to win matches. This was peculiarly unfortunate because, in Andy Irvine, Jim Renwick and Ian McGeechan, Scotland had running backs of unusual flair and brilliance.

Rutherford, then, began his international career in the middle of a losing streak, and it was, indeed, only in his seventh match for Scotland that he found himself on the winning side. It says some-thing for the often-maligned Scottish selectors that they kept faith with him; this was the time when England would chop and change their side with a reckless disregard for consistency. Indeed in his nine Calcutta Cup matches Rutherford played against five English number tens. Things have changed since, which is one reason for England's supremacy in the nineties.

In those days Rutherford was an indifferent kicker. He ran like a stag, he backed up brilliantly, but he was unable to control a game because he lacked that attribute which all the great fly-halves have possessed: the ability to put the ball where his forwards want it, and to perplex and tantalize opposing full-backs. He worked very hard on his kicking, and although, like most modern fly-halves, he never became completely two-footed, he did learn to use his left foot effectively, once dropping a goal left-footed for the South of Scotland against Australia.

Eventually he kicked as well as anyone in the game, destroying, for example, England's Dusty Hare in the 1984 Calcutta Cup. He was a master of every sort of kick: the garryowen, often directed into centre field from the blindside of a scrum; the rolling diagonal, the grubber and the chip. He made tries and disconcerted defences with all of them, one exquisite chip in Paris in 1987, which brought a try from Scott Hastings, staying bright in the memory.

He had wonderfully secure hands, and benefited from playing almost all his international rugby in partnership with Roy Laidlaw, of Jedforest, who also partnered him for the South of Scotland in the District Championship. Laidlaw was himself a splendidly gritty scrum-half, with an electric break, and an unselfish willingness to absorb punishment. They played together so often that Bill McLaren said they went together like ham and eggs, and that Laidlaw could find Rutherford in a darkened room. (He muttered that John was not the first person he would want to meet in those circumstances.) There were also four matches with his Selkirk partner, Gordon Hunter (Laidlaw being injured). Hunter was a very fine player, who was unlucky to be Laidlaw's contemporary.

I have said Rutherford was unlucky as far as the timing of the Lions tours went. He should have been taken to South Africa in 1980, raw as he still was. A try against England that year, when he cut clean through the defence to score under the posts, should have been enough to suggest how brilliantly he could have played on the hard grounds there. On the unhappy 1983 tour he had to be content with understudying Ollie Campbell, who had that year guided Ireland to a Triple Crown. All the same Campbell wasn't at his best on the tour, but kept his place as the man needed to kick goals. There was a case, as the Lions and Scotland coach Jim Telfer wished, for playing Rutherford at fly-half and Campbell at inside-centre, but the decision of the selection committee went against it.

Before then Rutherford had toured Australia with Scotland, and this experience was a great influence on his thinking and his development. Regarding Mark Ella as the finest fly-half he ever played against, he became an advocate of the Australian style in which the backs lie flat and vary the angle at which they take the ball. He developed the shuffle pass, while still employing the classic swing-away pass, when appropriate, to put the receiver outside his man.

In his first four seasons of international rugby Scotland were essentially a running team. A back division that might read Andy Irvine, Keith Robertson, David Johnston, Jim Renwick, Roger Baird, John Rutherford, Roy Laidlaw had speed, imagination, flair and panache. It lacked size, but every one of them delighted in running with the ball and beating his man by the old-fashioned (yet ever fresh and effective) means of sidestep, swerve, change of pace and dummy. All except the unlucky Baird (top try-scorer on the 1983 Lions tour) scored brilliant tries for Scotland – and Baird instigated the two most spectacular: the first try in the joyous 34–18 win at Cardiff in 1982, and the last in the 33–6 rout of England in 1986.

Things were a bit different in 1984, the year that saw Scotland's first Grand Slam since 1925. Irvine was injured and out of the side; so was Renwick. Rutherford adapted accordingly. He assumed more responsibility, and became the team's general, no longer playing instinctively or off-the-cuff, but with a calm authority and control. He had become the complete fly-half. Some English critics suggested that Scotland played 'kick-and-chase' rugby that year. Nevertheless they scored ten tries in the four matches, and Rutherford had a key part in at least six of them. His pick-up of a low pass, at ankle-height, to put the big Watsonian Euan Kennedy in for the second try against England was masterly.

He missed most of the unhappy 1985 season, when Scotland suffered a whitewash, on account of injury, and, since he was now thirty, some thought his international career might be coming to a close. These doubts intensified when the senior side was thrashed in that year's Scottish trial, and some, who should have known better, advised the selectors to dispense with Rutherford and Laidlaw. But the selectors kept faith, while introducing six new caps for the game with France, including the Hastings brothers.

That 1986 team was perhaps the best Scottish side of modern times, better than either the 1984 or 1990 Grand Slam winners.

Fortunate, perhaps, to beat France, they unluckily lost a great match in Cardiff despite scoring three tries to one (and David Sole will go to his grave convinced that he scored twice from short penalties, though the referee did not agree). Then they trounced England and beat Ireland to share the championship with France. The following year they lost a great match in Paris, and a poor one in appalling conditions at Twickenham. However, they proceeded to the first World Cup with justifiable confidence.

Before the team set off, Rutherford and a handful of other team members went on an unauthorized 'holiday' tour in Bermuda. In a practice game he suffered an injury to his anterior cruciate ligament, trying, ironically, to sidestep his Selkirk club-mate Iwan Tukalo. He arrived back at Edinburgh airport on crutches, but recovered sufficiently to travel to New Zealand. He played less than ten minutes of the first game against France, then with Scotland leading, thanks to a try by Derek White, he went down in a tackle; and that was the end of his international career, although he played a handful of games for Selkirk the following autumn before admitting the reality of his condition. It was a sad end, and who knows how different Scotland's fortunes in that World Cup might have been but for that ill-fated Bermuda trip?

The abiding memory is, first, of the elegance and grace of his running; right up to the end of his playing days he could cut open any defence. He read a game well, nearly always doing the right thing, and not passing on bad ball to the men outside him. In his great days his judgement of when to kick (and where and how), when to run and when to pass was well-nigh perfect. His defence was sound and he must have made more try-saving tackles than most fly-halves. He was a great runner in support of the ball-carrier, as good as anyone since Mike Gibson. He was at his best when the opposition was the best: on the international field or playing for Selkirk against Hawick, Gala or Heriot's. Sometimes, on lesser occasions, he could seem to lose interest. This was not for want of trying, but simply because the occasion was insufficiently stimulating. Curiously, he was not specially outstanding as a sevens player.

In any Scottish international seven of his time, Kelso's Andrew Kerr might have been preferred at fly-half – though there would always have been a strong case for playing Rutherford at centre.

Though he would sometimes run bad ball back into the forwards, partly on the ground that you might beat three or four players before you found anyone who could really tackle, he believed in making the ball do the work; the Selkirk and Scotland teams he played for relied on individual skills to beat a man and make an opening rather than on dreary crash-ball rugby. He exploited the blindside in masterly fashion and always looked for the chance to run ball out of defence.

Where does he rank among the great fly-halves? Of his contemporaries, only Mark Ella was clearly ahead, although it might be argued that Ella, genius though he was, never displayed Rutherford's willingness to take on defensive chores. The same might be said of Barry John and Phil Bennett, though Rutherford would be the first to admit that he did not have the knack of ghosting through apparently impregnable defences in their manner. He never perhaps touched the level that Barry John reached on the 1971 Lions tour. Then there is Mike Gibson, whom many would consider the greatest back of modern times; however, Gibson played perhaps his best rugby in the centre – outside John, indeed. Comparing players of different periods is difficult, even invidious – it's hard enough when they are contemporaries. All the same, I doubt if many would disagree, and certainly few Scots, if one ranked Rutherford among a select company of the truly outstanding number tens, along with Jackie Kyle, Cliff Morgan, Mike Gibson, Phil Hawthorn, Barry John, Phil Bennett, Mark Ella, Michael Lynagh and Jonathan Davies.

Through it all, John Rutherford has remained the same modest and delightful person he has always been. His modesty is such that it might even have retarded his career. It took him a long time to realize just how good he was. Yet his modesty helped him too: he was always willing to learn.

He is again living in Selkirk after several years of commuting from Edinburgh to the rugby club, and is a partner in a successful financial services firm. He coaches Selkirk, and has coached the South and various under-age Scottish representative sides, as well as the Scottish Students. All his teams are encouraged to play fifteen-man rugby and to run the ball, and all score spectacular tries. It may be that business commitments will prevent him from becoming the coach to the national side, although it is widely accepted that, with the possible exception of David Johnston, he is the best backs' coach in Scotland.

He is an example of everything that is best about rugby football, and the game has been the richer for his part in it. He has countless happy memories of his playing days, and so have all of us who were lucky enough to see him cut his elegant way through defences, or torment full-backs with his searching kicks.

Coming in From the Cold

TIAN STRAUSS

We'd dreamed of returning to Test rugby for years but, in the end, the lessons we learned as the first Springboks back after isolation proved harder than we could have imagined.

That first tour to France and England at the end of 1992, for example, on which we'd set off believing it was going to be difficult but essentially victorious, was probably the hardest lesson of them all. Club rugby in France is physically tough, with a high standard of skill, and the French loaded their regional invitational teams. I think some of the players faced us five or six times and every regional team seemed to contain at least a third of the French B team.

We were ill-prepared and naïve. Maybe, deep down, some of us believed the stories from our isolation years that the world crown would come our way as soon as we were allowed back in the fold, but we were disillusioned quickly. Team management was inexperienced. The coach, John Williams, and the rest of the management were well versed at provincial level, but they had no idea of the different standard expected internationally. Only the two veterans, Naas Botha and Danie Gerber, had played in the previous era. The rest of us were clueless.

Our travel arrangements were terrible. We had to spend ages in buses, driving up from Marseilles via Lille to Paris for memorably bum-numbing stretches of four and five hours at a time. The team manager hadn't – as Jannie Engelbrecht did subsequently – visited France beforehand to double check on our hotels. We'd end up

113

staying in the middle of nowhere, unable to find training facilities and spending hours looking for suitable practice grounds. You couldn't blame management for this: they didn't know what they had to do with regard to these matters.

Come match time, we didn't cover ourselves in glory. At that stage we had nothing that could be called a playing pattern. Everything turned around Naas – give him the ball and he'd do the rest. That worked a treat in provincial rugby back home, but at this level it wasn't enough.

But we learned – we spent the next couple of seasons continuously learning. We observed the commitment of the typical French player, the tempo at which the team played international rugby. Especially in that first Test at Lille, which we won, mainly thanks to poor place-kicking by Sebastien Viars for France. We were very lucky that time – I remember spending the last twenty minutes defending desperately. We were unable to dictate the pace of the match, unable to slow it down and even less able to speed it up, which left us waiting to see what France were going to come up with and trying to stop them doing it.

The sheer speed of it took us by surprise and my eyes were opened by the way every man jack of them – prop, hooker, lock – was a real player, a ball player. It wasn't like we'd become used to at home, with props just scrumming. Their ball skills, from regional sides upwards to the real McCoy, made an eye-opener for what we'd still have to do to become the best.

On to England and my first Test try. I remember that day well – it drizzled a bit in London and when we got to Twickenham there were a few demonstrators outside the ground. They didn't achieve much – neither unsettled us, nor speeded up the process of democratizing South Africa. We had an absolutely magnificent first half. Naas sank a wonderful drop goal and everything went right for us. He kicked a ball out close to the England goal line and the line-out was a shambles. I fell back and called for a pass from Garth Wright, dropped my head and barged through.

I had a vague sense of being at Twickenham, of scoring a try for the Springboks and of it being my first Test score, but the feeling only properly sank in a day later. I wished I could have the moment again, to savour it fully, but I can only remember Danie Gerber embracing me, happier about it than I was. By the time I had fully absorbed what had happened, the second half was already over. England took control and won 33–16. What they really showed up in our game was that we weren't a team at all. Everybody tried to do his own thing, with nobody able to express himself in a team context.

France came to South Africa the next year and our luck had not changed. We were poor in the first Test, but hung on for a draw. In the second Test I felt we were on top. But whereas poor place-kicking by Viars had helped in Lille a few months earlier, this time the boot was on the other foot. Thierry Lacroix had been in poor place-kicking form all tour, but at Ellis Park nothing went wrong for him. Theo van Rensburg missed two vital shots at goal and we lost the series by a single point.

So it goes. A few weeks later, however, we tasted real glory. I loved Australia. We started out in Perth, which reminded me a lot of my home, Cape Town. Friendly people and then the wonderful Swan River. And at Orange, near Sydney, one of the all-time great after-match functions. Farming people, everybody in their jeans and boots and not a pretension in sight. Sydney I loved as well, and especially that first Test against the Wallabies. I think that was probably the highlight of my international career. Our plans came off for really the first time and we were all 100 per cent committed. We'd exploited their blindside, where the lock Garrick Morgan was unsuccessfully revamped as flank. It was immensely gratifying.

In the end, though, they were the better side and took the series deservedly, but we were on the up and up. And then the selectors decided to experiment wildly for our tour to Argentina later that year.

It was unnecessary and, with hindsight, foolish. It's a good thing to blood young players, but with a tour to New Zealand a year later we should have used the opportunity to strengthen our core.

There was, yet again, wholesale chopping and changing for the tour to New Zealand.

The Argentinians at home are a much tougher proposition than they are on tour. Their club sides are very good and for the most part their referees do their bit to make your games really hard. With the class of player they have in Argentina, they ought to be a world power. They remind me a little of France a few years ago, before Pierre Berbizier took over the reins and instilled some discipline into the national side. They're six or nix players – when they're good they're great, but when you apply pressure relentlessly, they lapse back into every-man-for-himself mode.

Of course, there was also that match against Tucumán. Ever since our return there seemed to be one match like it per year – there was the battle of Marseilles in '92, then Tucumán and in '94 there was Neath. I watched Marseilles, but threw my share of punches in the other two. I hate dirty play, but these were occasions when, if you turned the other cheek, they'd just punch you twice as hard on it. We were forewarned about Tucumán. Also that they based their success on their scrummaging. We'd decided that we were going to take them on in the scrums and they didn't like that. The fighting started with a head-butt on our Keith Andrews in the first scrum and we stood there exchanging blows for five or ten minutes. I was captain that night and told the guys that that was that for the fighting: you're allowed to hit back, but now we must play them off their feet. And we did.

But it was all rather unbelievable. If you tackled their full-back, he'd spit at you and start swearing. It was difficult to concentrate on the rugby, but we scored some great tries.

At The Gnoll a year later we were lucky to escape with a victory, having allowed ourselves to be somewhat put out by the dirty play. Afterwards there were ridiculous suggestions that we'd set off the Neath boys by claiming to have slept with their wives and mothers – some of the guys said they wouldn't even know how to say that in English!

But I digress. I quite enjoyed Argentina '93. Buenos Aires, such a great town – and the way the people live. In the middle of this immense city with its 8 million plus inhabitants, the people are as friendly and relaxed as any in a small town. What's important to them is communication. Money matters aren't as important as life itself. I like that dedication to the quality of life.

I'd spent a summer or two in Italy for much the same reason. Rugby-wise, my Italian experience wasn't much help when it came to life on the international stage. I didn't go there to improve my rugby but to experience Italy, see how they live, how they eat. And there I picked up the lesson that life's quality is much more important than what you've got stashed in the bank. They have a lot in common with the Argentinians and I'd advise every young player who can to go to Italy. Not for your rugby, just to broaden the mind. But that's by the way.

After our tour to Argentina, England came over to South Africa and played poorly right up to that first Test. Before the game I got the feeling that none of us took them as seriously as they deserved and if you don't respect an opponent, you're asking for it. It was also the first time we played after the democratic elections. We were emotionally more affected by meeting President Mandela than they were. Democracy made our lives as international rugby players much easier. On that first trip to France and England, we'd get our fair share of insults, but the further down the road we moved, the easier it became. In particular, it was never pleasant standing out there listening to the other team singing their national anthem and not being able to respond. It touched you, especially being away from home. Being able to sing again has improved the situation a lot. That first time, however, the whole thing made it somewhat trickier out on the field.

But I don't want to make excuses. The England forwards were magnificent. After twenty minutes they'd already effectively played us out of the game and, try as we might, we couldn't recover. I spent the second Test in the stand and watched the 'Boks pull off that great recovery and then it was time to pack the bags for New Zealand.

New Zealand. Still the greatest of dreams for a South African rugby player. It's a must, the ultimate rugby tour. Everybody knows the game. The old lady in the pub is as likely as anybody to be an authority on it and can tell you everything you want to know about the 'Boks of '56 or '65.

The atmosphere before a Test is like nothing else. And the rugby is hard. Sometimes we'd run out against a team that wouldn't strike us as physically impressive, but the moment we made contact we'd know that these are guys for whom it's a religion. They give everything. Every match is a struggle to win, thanks to this determination. The circumstances make it difficult to play – it's raining the whole time, the fields are soft. If you took the New Zealanders and put them in ideal playing conditions, like those in South Africa (give or take the odd quagmire, as in the France–South Africa World Cup game), they'd be the best players in the world – and I still say that even after South Africa's victory in the 1995 World Cup.

Missing those first Tests against New Zealand and Australia when we returned from isolation didn't trouble me too much. Jannie Breedt was still around and still the first choice as number eight. However, earlier that year we played trials for a tour to Romania and Italy that never came off. I was picked as number one.

I would have liked to have made my Test début at home in South Africa, but I knew my chance was going to come. Anyway, those first two matches weren't resounding successes. The first one, against New Zealand, made the world sit up and take notice. But a week later, at Newlands, Australia gave us notice of what had become required at Test level. I wasn't on the field for that defeat of 26–3 so it couldn't have harmed my reputation any!

Anyway, not having been in the side to begin with, it wasn't such a disappointment. Being dropped after that disastrous first Test against England in 1994, that hurt. I didn't play well, but neither did any of the other forwards or, for that matter, anybody on the team. I'd played ten Tests on the run, at least reasonably well in all of them and very well in a few. To be dropped after one poor performance, with nobody else distinguishing themselves either, that was unfair and it disappointed me more than somewhat.

Still, that's life as a Test rugby player and to wrap up the topic of disappointments I'd have to say that losing my Test place on the 'Boks tour of Scotland, Wales and Ireland towards the end of '94 took the cake. I'd regained my Test place on that hard, hard tour of New Zealand earlier in the year, losing it for the third Test and regaining it when Argentina came to tour South Africa before the tour to Britain. It went well against the Pumas, but I came off injured in the second Test. I had to sit out the first two matches in Britain – those against Cardiff and Wales A – but for the third one, against Llanelli at Stradey Park, I was ready. I came down with flu earlier in the week, but by Thursday I was training properly and not feeling any after-effects. I told our coach Kitch Christie that I was rarin' to go, but he said it would be taking unnecessary chances to play so soon after the flu. He added that there was no rush – still plenty of time to prove myself – and I felt reassured.

As things turned out, that match against Llanelli was the last one where players were mixed and matched. After that, we'd settled into a Wednesday team and a Saturday team. I played in that unpleasant match against Neath at The Gnoll and Rudolf Straeuli played in the magnificent win over Swansea at St Helen's.

I was quite cheesed off. I went on tour as number one and went home as number two, without ever getting a chance to show my mettle with the better team. If I'd had a run with the Saturday side and Christie had decided after that that I wasn't good enough, I would have accepted it. But, as happens on lots of tours, the Wednesday teams drew the short straw. There were weeks when we'd played tougher opposition than the Saturday guys did. I think management erred there – on tour you should pick your sides according to the level of the opposition faced.

All the attention, in the meantime, was heaped on the Saturday team and the dirt trackers had to make the best of their situation, which, under the circumstances, wasn't much.

I ended up coaching the outcasts, who felt that they were no longer in the running and were terribly demotivated. It ended with us laughing at one of the guys' rather bitter chirp that we had had absolutely nothing to worry about – there was no way they could drop us from the Wednesday team. Mainly because there was nowhere to drop us to.

If you wind up becoming so negative, your chances of success become rather dim. As a result, the British tour was, for me personally, a low point. But I'll be back . . .

Halcyon Days

RAY GRAVELL

'Perhaps my best years are gone ... but I wouldn't want them back. Not with the fire in me now.' So wrote that Celtic man of words Samuel Beckett. I tend to agree with Mr Beckett, but there are times when I do yearn for a day or two of bygone years, especially when thinking in particular of Welsh rugby. Yes indeed, during the last ten or fifteen years, success seems to have bypassed us and found a comfortable resting place just beyond Offa's Dyke.

Now I wouldn't dream of denying our neighbours the praise and adulation that comes in the wake of victory, and goodness knows they've had plenty of reason to celebrate, with Triple Crowns and Grand Slams and so on, but it wasn't always the case. Oh, no. So please bear with me while I reminisce, or lament even, on a glorious past that I remember so well.

Through my mind's eye I'll hurdle back over the decades to my very first encounter with rugby football or, rather, with a rugby ball. The early fifties, Christmas time and a wide-eyed boisterous child of four, enthusiastically tearing open a carefully wrapped parcel, to find inside this rather odd-shaped ball with a distinctive smell. Funny how some things tend to stay with you, and even now, forty years on, whenever I see a rugby ball (even on TV) my sense of smell immediately springs into action.

There is something intoxicating about leather. Synthetic balls? You can keep them! Give me leather every time. Anyway, that was an initial introduction into the wondrous, mystical and most certainly magical world of rugby.

121

Geographically I live in the Gwendraeth Valley in Dyfed, West Wales: a predominantly Welsh-speaking area, once the very prosperous domain of King Coal, and the proud workforce that dug deep and hauled out 'Black Gold', so that an élite few could live the life of luxury, while the majority kept on digging and dreaming. Still the bonds of hardship are unbreakable: work hard, play hard. They did. One such man was my father, Jack Gravell. He worked underground in Pentremawr colliery in Pontyberem, and also played for the local rugby team, a tough, uncompromising forward. It was he, along with my uncle Ron (my mother's brother), who took me to see my first rugby match.

Now I can honestly say I don't remember a thing about this occasion – apparently I was more interested in the swings and roundabouts at Park Stephens in Cydweli than the rugby that was being played by the grown-ups just a few yards away. But, still, it was an introduction to a sport that was to play a big part in my life and still does to this day.

From humble beginnings I slowly moved on to bigger things – and they don't come any bigger than Llanelli Rugby Football Club. There is an old saying that 'To be born Welsh is to be born privileged.' I'd like to add that to be born ten miles from Stradey Park, Llanelli, is indeed a bonus. How well I remember going to Stradey with my father and his mining pals to watch the Scarlets play: to a young boy standing on the touchline, they all seemed like giants hell bent on knocking the living daylights out of one another. I was hooked. I'd risen to the bait, and eagerly awaited the weekly journeys, courtesy of an Eynon's double-decker bus, on the road that led to Llanelli.

As my interest in the Scarlets increased, so did my own ambitions. Rugby football took over, and luckily, as kids in the village of Mynydd-y-Garreg (where I grew up, and still live), we were encouraged to let our imaginations run wild. We played regularly, morning, noon and night, regularly beating England by a hundred points or so, freedom of expression being of paramount importance!

Now that's something that modern-day coaches could well instil into the minds of their players (and themselves).

My father always kept a proud, watchful eye over me and encouraged me, telling me of the Welsh players that were his heroes, Bleddyn Williams, Jack Matthews, Cliff Morgan, R. H. Williams, and proudly recalling that he'd often played against the great Carwyn James. To a young lad this was thrilling stuff and consequently his heroes became my heroes, his dreams my dreams (and one particular dream that I was to fulfil in later life, more so his than mine).

Sadly, my father died when I was fourteen, and my mother took over the dual role of parenthood, for which I will be eternally grateful, for without her guiding influence, support and encouragement, what was to follow would certainly not have materialized.

For me and a few other boys as well schooldays at Carmarthen Grammar were not so much academic as sporting days, mostly athletics, cricket and rugby. Whereas my father had always had ambitions of my being an outside-half and 100-metre sprinter, reality had me developing into a high hurdler and budding inside-half-cum-centre-threequarter. When I left school at seventeen, my name had been mentioned to the powers that be at Stradey Park, Llanelli, and I was invited to join their youth team, which I did. This was the beginning of an adventure that I still haven't fully appreciated, but will do so I'm sure in the fullness of time.

It was 1969 and Llanelli RFC were about to embark on an historic and revolutionary rugby journey that was to rock the rugby world. New ideas would be implemented in coaching and a level of physical fitness achieved that few other clubs would surpass. Exciting, innovative times and the beginning of a golden era. Imagine what it was like for a teenager like myself to find himself involved with the club that as a boy he had supported, and whose players he had idolized. There I was on the same training ground as players who were already household names: Delme Thomas, Phil Bennett, Roy Mathias and Norman Gale.

That first year with Llanelli Youth proved a fruitful one indeed:

three Welsh Youth caps, and a lasting friendship with one Gareth Jenkins. Gareth was a flank-forward, our captain and also the Welsh Youth captain. He went on to play for the senior side, toured and played for Wales in a Test match in Japan, and seemingly had a glittering career ahead of him as a player, until a severe knee injury brought his playing involvement to a premature end. Happily he is still a force, not only with Llanelli but with Welsh rugby, and will be more so, I think, in future years. I was in good company. Good fortune came my way, in that I avoided serious injury, and I played my first game for the senior side, the legendary Scarlets, at only eighteen.

The training methods implemented during the late sixties and early seventies were both spartan and scientific, courtesy of a giant of a man: Professor of Physical Education at Bath University, former paratrooper and Olympic pentathlete, Tom Hudson. When Tom said, 'Run,' you bloody well ran! We ran up mountains and sand dunes, tackled trees, pounded the roads, lifted weights, swam and kept on running. We were the fittest squad of players in Great Britain, and the fitter I was, the more confident I became and this was reflected in my game – coupled with the fact that I was now playing alongside some of the best in the world.

It was a strange feeling to be on first-name terms with people who to me were heroes. One in particular I must mention, the great Delme Thomas, second-row forward, three times British Lion and captain of Wales. Delme had been a favourite of mine ever since I had seen a photograph of him on the back page of the *Western Mail* when he had been selected to tour with the British Lions to New Zealand in 1966. I had said a tentative 'Hello' to him once in Carmarthen town, and in return received a broad smile of approval. But now, here I was not only in the same changing room as my hero but actually playing in the team that he captained.

Some people would say that heroes are not what they seem to be, and through no fault of their own, because it is we, the fans, who put them up there on a pedestal. Not so with Delme, for to me the man was much more than the rugby player: he was a gentleman, a kindly man, and I can proudly say that my hero became my friend and we are still bosom pals. Delme was a legend, and there were a few legends jogging around at Stradey Park at the same time. Characters, too, were in abundance, and none more so than our physiotherapist Hubert Peel, known affectionately as Bert to one and all. He was a former coal miner, still spitting out the mining souvenirs while running on to the pitch with the magic sponge. Always smiling, always joking, he loved life and lived it to the full. I'm of the firm belief that Bert knew more about psychology a quarter of a century ago than do today's professional psychologists. I remember one instance: I'd just crashed into my opposing centre, a crunching tackle which resulted in my needing some treatment. On came Bert, put his bag down beside me and said, 'What's the matter, Gravell bach?' 'It's my shoulder, Bert,' I said. 'OK, stay still,' and he pulled out the magic sponge and rubbed it on my forehead. 'Bert,' I said, 'it's my shoulder that hurts.' 'That may be so,' said Bert, 'but the problem is up here,' as he continued to rub my head.

I think he was right. It was Bert who was the first to tell me that one day I would play for Wales. I didn't believe him at the time but, as was so often the case, Bert was right and I was wrong.

He will long be remembered at Stradey Park, and is still sadly missed. Five feet tall in his stockinged feet, 'A big man on short legs' – a great man.

While on the subject of great men, one name above all others is instantly identified throughout the rugby world as that of the maestro, the late great Carwyn James. Carwyn was a man of vision, a cultured man, a thinking man, a Llanelli man. He was coach to the successful Lions side of 1971, the first Lions team to win a Test series against the All Blacks. When they returned triumphantly home, Carwyn was acclaimed and acknowledged as a rugby authority. The true sadness was that he was never given the opportunity of coaching the Welsh side.

At the time Welsh rugby was governed by men who wore dark

glasses at night – but not at Stradey Park: Carwyn was given the freedom and authority to conduct the rugby affairs of Llanelli RFC. We loved him. He had a way with words (in Welsh and in English); he understood people, though perhaps not himself at all times; he could handle people. Like Bert, he knew a thing or two about psychology. He had the ability to make you think that you were better than you were. When we were playing against Coventry in the early seventies, my task was to mark a centre by the name of David Duckham. Quite a task for a young unknown like myself, but here's what Carwyn told me in the changing room during the team talk ten minutes before the start of the game.

'Ray, you're better than Duckham. Go out there and prove it.' I knew that Carwyn wasn't actually telling the truth and so did the other boys, but I believed him, and that belief was reflected in the way I played that afternoon.

He had charisma and an aura that made you feel all the better for knowing him. What was his finest hour? Well, he had so many, but I think that the satisfaction he felt after Llanelli beat New Zealand 9–3 in October 1972 was total. He had tasted huge success with the British Lions, but this time it was his team, Llanelli RFC, against the might of a nation and the mightiest rugby nation of them all, New Zealand, and furthermore we won with style, and Carwyn was also a stylish man. He felt passionately about rugby football, and enjoyed to the full the drama and poetic presence that one finds in a rugby match.

They were halcyon, heady days in West Wales during the seventies. The mercurial Phil Bennett wove his particular magic, and enthralled the crowds with his artistic majesty – Roy Bergiers, J. J. Williams, Tom David, Derek Quinnell and Barrie Llewellyn and the names just keep on rolling. The more I look back on those days the happier and better they seem. Luck was also on my side, and in January 1975 in Paris I fulfilled not only my dream but also that of my late father: I played for Wales. Strangely enough, while realizing that dream I also shattered it, and in so doing felt my father's presence at Parc des Princes when we beat France 25–10.

126

I felt a surge of energy, not only physically but psychologically, that I had never experienced before or since.

While looking back, one realizes that there is a solid base for the future. Rugby is ever changing and we must move with the times. Inevitably rugby will become totally professional for the world is a commercial and professional world. What we in Wales must do is to set the pace of change. Be innovative, positive and have vision; for to have vision is to be bold and adventurous. It worked for us in the past, so let's get on that highway to the future together; for I think that slumbering dragon is about to wake with a thunderous roar: '*Cymru am byth.*'

Putting the Boot In

JON CALLARD

The changing room was silent. I sat there with my head in my hands, wondering what on earth I had done. Well, I knew what I'd done, but why? I couldn't understand it. The kicks hadn't been difficult, it wasn't wet, it wasn't windy, it was a perfect spring day, and I just couldn't come to terms with the disastrous result of my miserable kicking. Bath had just lost to Saracens 9–7 in a league game and the penalties I had missed totalled five. If only one of those five had gone over we would have won the game and probably the league title as well. I was totally devastated by what had happened, not because I had missed five kicks at goal but because I had failed when it really mattered. I had let down my team-mates.

The direness of the situation was driven home to me as my fellow players' expressions became very visible. Jack Rowell, the Bath coach, gave voice to these expressions by announcing to our captain, Andy Robinson, that I was banned from kicking and that I would not be allowed to kick again for Bath. While he made these observations mainly in jest, I knew, deep inside, that he was right. We had lost the game because I had failed in my responsibility to the team and the club. It was a public rebuke that left me in turmoil about my mental ability to kick goals. My thinking had been shrouded with doubt. The thought of missing another goal in front of my team-mates had put me off and banished any dreams I had of kicking winning goals in injury time to win games.

I think what also infuriated me was the ease with which I could kick goals while practising on the training ground. It was effortless. I could obtain an aesthetic awareness of and satisfaction from my ability to kick; but on the field at Saracens it just disappeared. Whatever skill I thought I had just seemed to disintegrate and was left in the changing room on that dreadful day.

It was to haunt me for twelve months and in that time I never attempted another kick. Not in a game, not in training and certainly not in my mind. Kicking was something I never envisaged doing again. I remember Jon Webb talking about goal-kicking while he was in the England squad. He claimed it was a completely separate aspect of the game and could not and should not be integrated into an individual's play. A person who is kicking has to rid himself of the rugby mind and the state of the game in which he is playing and don the mind of goal-kicker. A new identity if you like. Cool, focused and with a calculated technique that has been practised a million times before. It is the combination of the physical and mental being in perfect unison with each other. Too tense in the mind, too tense in the body and the legs. Too lax in the mind, too lax in the legs and carelessness ensues. Thinking back to my efforts in the Saracens game this was not me, but I was now ready to try again.

Six o'clock in the morning. The alarm was bidding me to get up and the first session of training was only an hour away. It meant being at Whitchurch leisure centre for a kicking session with Stuart Barnes, Jon Webb and our tutor Dave Alred, known to us as Hank the Yank. Barnesy gave him this nickname because of his use of American football expressions in our training sessions. 'Down the tube,' he would bellow, or 'Right on the money' or 'That's a turn-over' or 'It's chasing off your foot.' He brought these across the water with him and they annoyed us intensely. After the first session I attended I thought I'd stumbled across a senile old player who had just been let loose from some American kicking academy. Kicking to what purpose? Barnesy, Webby and I hadn't a clue. Nevertheless, it was these sessions that gently rehabilitated me back into the art of goal-kicking. The mental work was to rebuild the channels that had been demolished in my mind. A set rhythm, a focus, a technique and, most important, a plan that was to eliminate any negative thoughts, this last being the most important and the most difficult because without it goal-kicking will always be unsuccessful.

The physical technique was the easy part, calculating the stride length and the best possible angle to approach the ball. Every individual is different, and the angle at which each one makes contact with the ball is peculiar to him. It is a question of playing around with the technique in front of the video and watching it over and over again.

Once you're happy with this technique you can progress to stage two and this is more demanding. It is all about being able to feel the ball as you make contact with it at the right tempo, which should produce a sweet 'pop' sound, rather than a 'splat' or a 'slap', which indicate the strike is out of timing. This aspect of our training caused great amusement to the domestic staff of the leisure centre. Balls were flying everywhere, apart from through the middle of the posts, with the three of us taking great delight in pronouncing 'Great strike!', 'Lovely pop' or 'That's right on the money!' It was, however, a serious exercise that develops one's inner feel for kicking the ball. Get this right and you're a third of the way to being a successful kicker. Hank used to have us listening to each other's kicks, trying to distinguish between a sweet and a sour one. We graded each other's pops with a mark out of ten. No one ever got a full ten as we felt this was perfection, and perfection could never be reached. Not even the great Jon Webb could achieve that.

I could understand this and found it easy in the environment of the practice field. I was satisfied with the progress in my technique. I developed a sequence that I could use in games as well as training. Four paces back, three to the side, stop, half-step back, stutter, three paces forward, then strike the ball. So much for the sequence, but the rhythm and the tempo were also important, and were based on counting, or picking off a series of numbers. I devised a secret routine, counting these numbers in a way that would give me the right tempo. One two three four stop, three two one stop, half-pace stutter, one two three strike.

The problem was of controlling this system and dismissing any negative thoughts that would enter my head, like, 'Oh, this is an easy kick' or 'I really must get this because what happens if I miss?' I needed a positive statement to occupy my mind and push the negative influences to the back. Hank came up with the notion of the 'line – spot – follow through'. This was to be said before approaching the ball. My mind had three clear things on which to concentrate. The first was the line created by the direction of the foot, the second, the point of contact which the foot was to make with the ball, and the third, the direction of the foot as it followed through after making contact with the ball. It was clear and precise, my mind was totally occupied and now, in theory, the fundamentals of a successful kick were in place. Sadly, in practice, this was not always the case.

By this time Jon Webb had become number one full-back for Bath and England. I was practising my new technique in second-team matches and at the start I regularly failed to hit the target. I was, however, coming to terms with holding my body and mind in a relaxed but focused state. This could only be achieved by kicking regularly. Gradually my success rate improved because my mind and body became used to performing under pressure. It was something that could not be practised on the training field. I was contrasting my current performance against a disastrous game when playing for Newport in 1985 against Fiji: I had to make a kick from 40 metres to win the game; I missed and we lost 7–6. Despite my progress, however, these techniques and principles had not yet been tried in the pressurized atmosphere of a Bath first-team league game.

Jon Webb retired before the start of the 1993–4 season. Stuart Barnes was struggling with what seemed to be an irreparable back injury in a build-up to a Northampton game in the Courage League. It was an important game: the leagues were only a week old and Northampton were coming to Bath to show that they were worthy contenders for the division one title. Barnesy's injury was quite alarming, not only to the coaching staff but to the servants who produced the business on the field. The barrel was suffering and didn't we know about it! Doctors, physios, osteopaths and shrinks were summoned and each had their own prognosis. I suspected that Barnesy would play but that he would delegate some of his responsibility. It played on my mind all week. Would I be taking the kicks again in a first-division match? What were the stakes if I did? It was a huge mental challenge to come to terms with.

At Downside I would suddenly drift away from my teaching duties and think about a ball missing the post and sailing by. I suppose it was like a migraine: it would build up and build up and I would try physically to shake it off. I don't know why, but I was convincing myself that I did not want to kick again and face what I had faced before, despite my current good form in the second team. The prospect of missing kicks and the crowd holding me accountable and my team-mates being deflated seemed daunting.

On the way to the ground from the team hotel, a long-standing supporter stopped me in the street just outside the main gates. He had overheard some of the other players saying that Barnesy would start but J.C. would do all the kicking to relieve him from some of the pressure. 'Look,' he said, 'I know it's none of my business but I just want to say something before you go out on to the field. The objective is still the same. The method and the techniques are still the same, and even more important the field and the posts are exactly the same. It doesn't matter whether you are at Twickenham, Downside or on the Rec, the aim is still the same. The ball has got to go through the posts irrespective of the situation of the game and the ground you're on. Every time you kick you've got to think that you're on the training ground, that you're an individual who is on his own.'

He was absolutely right; never has such a statement had such an impact. It was clear that nothing should interfere with my ability to kick goals. OK, perhaps the conditions could have a bearing, but that should be it. I accepted his observations and, what is more important, I accepted the responsibility that lay ahead. However, his theory was not enough on its own. I added my own objectives for this game, and those were to concentrate on the contact and the timing. I felt that if I focused on these two fundamental points I would worry less about my role. It proved a successful day but I was unconscious of how successful it had been. I had scored twenty-four of our thirty-four points. It did not sink in what had happened. Yes, I was pleased with the outcome of six out of six, but what was really pleasing was that I developed an awareness of kicking a rugby ball in a pressure match while completely controlling my attitude and technique. When further reflecting on my performance, I became anxious that my success should not be put down to its being 'one of those days' when sportsmen claim everything just went right for them, but when asked why, can offer no coherent explanation. When further pressed you start to hypothesize with ridiculous and superstitious reasons. I made breakfast for my wife this morning, I put £10 in the collection tin before the game. I was courteous to the driver who nearly ran me off the road. It's all twaddle but, all the same, it had been my day.

I was becoming uncomfortable that now everyone expected that every time I kicked the ball it would bring fruitful rewards. It did. I hit a purple patch in what was the most important part of my rugby career to date. England needed a goal-kicking full-back and my name had been put forward. Jack Rowell claimed that my form was 'breathtaking' and urged me to retire while I was on top or, conversely, share the medication that I was supposed to be taking with the rest of the lads in the changing room. Knowing Jack, he probably wanted me to do the two things simultaneously.

The first of my hurdles was playing for the South and South West against the All Blacks at Redruth. The game was a great opportunity not only for me but for the division. As divisional champions, we were taking on one of the best sides in the world. They even paid the South West a compliment in playing their Test side, to show that they were not taking the game lightly.

Unfortunately for the South West it was a tremendous effort but not quite good enough. Had I had my kicking boots on we would have won the game comfortably. Not for the first time I had been offered a big opener and I blew it. I missed four kicks, but what was more disconcerting was the way in which I missed them. Sadly, I have no recollection of what happened or why it went that way. I do not even remember the ones I did kick. Everything that I had developed so carefully over the previous two years went out of the window. The strike, the tempo, the mental imagery just disappeared. Why? It seemed the more I tried the worse it got.

Although by the end of the match I had controlled myself and become aware of my role, it was after I had kicked only two out of six that I started to feel the ball again. Perhaps I tried too hard because I was desperate to impress the selectors. Also the conditions did not help. I mentioned earlier that the weather and the state of the pitch are the only external factors that affect a good kicker. That day the pitch was awful and, while this cannot excuse my performance, it was a pity that such an important match had to be played at such a venue. Not because it was in Cornwall but because the facilities at Redruth were not up to a game of such magnitude. It would have been better to have played at a football stadium where the pitch was level. The ground had an obvious slant towards one of the corners – in fact, a gradient sign would have been helpful on the 22, warning you of the severe slope ahead. Yet although the ground was sadly lacking, the crowd were fantastic and the support they gave was tremendous. I am only sorry that we did not produce a win as a fitting reward for their enthusiasm that day. I'm not saying that it is not possible to kick well on such a ground, only that those factors affected me and my confidence, and gave me problems in my approach to such an important game in my career.

It was a great opportunity missed. My dreams of representing my country were gone – at least I thought they were. I had had the chance but I had thrown it away and all I could salvage was the experience and the determination that if I was ever placed in the same situation again it would not have the same outcome. This setback was not going to defeat me. An aberration like a blip on a computer, a lapse in power, caused a loss of memory and affected my performance. That week I went to the training ground every day and rehearsed and rehearsed every kick again and again, and each time I shouted out loud the sequence of instructions.

Deep inside I knew where the problem lay: anxiety had got the better of me and it was not going to happen again. I set myself targets and rewards for the week. Each training session I gave myself nine kicks at goal. If I achieved seven out of nine I rewarded myself with three kicks from a greater distance. If I kicked two out of three of these kicks I would give myself the ultimate reward, which was a final kick from the half-way line. Kicking from the half-way line was the ultimate reward. Failing at any stage to reach my target would result in my having to start again and keep starting again until I reached the half-way line. It was a good way of stimulating a feeling of success and of kicking well because once I had reached the 50-metre mark I had done well, irrespective of the successful attempt at the half-way line.

The following week I was given the opportunity again to prove myself as a prospective international kicker. I was selected to play for the England A side at Gateshead. This time it was at a venue conducive to good rugby and good kicking. I spent thirty minutes each day going through the mental imagery of goal-kicking. All my successful goals went through the post. I played them back in my mind. I recorded the sound of the ball as it left my foot and I watched its flight through the air. I was playing back to myself and proving to myself that no matter what kick I had to take I could handle it. I would be totally focused. I decided that I was going to adopt the strategy of having just two words and using them as I prepared to kick: spot and strike. I repeated these words in my mind and used them while I was setting up the ball to kick it. The sequence of instructions that I had developed in the past was still present in my mind, as this is something that happens instinctively. I did not have to remind myself of them.

As the game progressed, I was kicking well but the success rate was not good. Only four out of seven, but I was pleased with the feel and the timing that I was creating. The strike was good and the sound being produced when foot met ball was satisfying. Mysteriously, however, the crowd were at odds with my satisfaction and some elements within it turned on me. I was aware dispassionately of what was being said but it did not affect me. It was only on reflection that I realized that I was starting to control my inner self.

The experiences at Redruth and Gateshead made me a better player and a better goal-kicker because I had been subjected to disappointment and could now handle it when faced with it. Although my success rate had not been good, and probably if I had kicked all my goals we would have won both games, I was still satisfied. I had come through another bad experience with my mind positive and disciplined. Not everyone agreed with me, however. As I left the ground with my club-mate Nigel Redman, one little lad said to his friend, 'That's Jon Callard. Go and get his autograph.' His young friend riposted, 'Not likely! He's fucking rubbish. He couldn't kick the skin off a rice pudding.'

I thought about it all the way back to Bath but I felt I had come through the ordeal intact and was grateful for the experience. Despite the important lessons I had learned I had a sinking feeling that I had not shown myself to be good enough in these matches as a reliable kicker and that the opportunity for playing for my country had gone. It was the closest, I felt, that I was going to come and the chance would not arise again.

The squad for the New Zealand game was being announced the following Tuesday. I thought about being selected but could not convince myself that I would be. Two full-backs, however, had been named: Jon Callard and Ian Hunter. I thought that I was slightly ahead of Ian Hunter because at that time England was looking for a full-back who could kick goals. Ian Hunter was an exceptional footballer but he did not kick for his club. Suddenly, I was back in the reckoning with a chance of fulfilling a life-long dream of playing for my country in a full international at Twickenham.

Geoff Cooke read out the team the following Sunday morning

at the Petersham Hotel behind closed doors with just the squad assembled in the room. Twenty-three of us prayed that our names would be called out. My name was first on the list as Geoff started with fifteen and worked downwards. I didn't hear another name. Was I still asleep? Had the two disappointments at Redruth and Gateshead been a dream? Perhaps they had just been forgotten. When my mind was able to take it in I thought it was a brave decision by the selectors, but because they were looking for a goal-kicking full-back, I thought it was the correct one. I had proved that I could kick goals in club matches and had a successful record for my club. The past experience of the South West and the A game had had a positive effect on me. I felt that some of the pressure had now been lifted off my shoulders.

I was, of course, entrusted with the responsibility of kicking the goals for the side. It was something that I had come to terms with and as a consequence enjoyed. The magnitude of the occasion did not cross my mind. I was determined to enjoy it and nothing would spoil it.

On the morning of the game I practised my routine on the third floor of the hotel. It consisted of focusing on a point on the carpet and making sure I got the run just right. I felt that if I got this right the strike would follow naturally. It was not until this private session that I stumbled on something that would prove vital in my role as a goal-kicker. I adopted a stance that allowed me to lean over the ball before reversing away from it. This exaggerated my knee forward and enabled me to feel the position I was trying to obtain when striking the ball. In theory, however, my head was in front of the ball and my eyes focused on a point about a metre ahead of it. Until now I had been looking straight down at the ball and having my head right over the top of it, so that when I came to kick it my foot would slide underneath it and lift it unnecessarily; the loss of power would cause the ball to fall some way short of the target. Also, in this private session, I found a comfortable position for the non-kicking foot, which allowed me to bring the other leg through comfortably without it being obstructed.

Although I had never tried to lean forward like this on the training field, and certainly not in a game, I was so confident that it did
not worry me. I decided on the bus on the way to the pitch that I
would try out my theory before the match. Sometimes we go out
to warm up and get a feel of the atmosphere. I thought I would
use this time to see if my theory had been right.

At Twickenham, half an hour before kick-off, I placed the ball
down and gave myself a target to aim at. I also placed bits of card
on the ground in an attempt to see if my stride pattern could get
me in the strike position that I had developed in the hotel. It was
spot on: three times I tried it and three times I got my non-kicking
foot into the planned position. I thought at this stage, twenty
minutes before kick-off, that I was not going to experiment any
more. I was at ease with myself and confident that I could handle
anything that was given to me.

It was fourteen minutes into the game when the first penalty was
awarded to England, 40 metres out and slightly to the right of
the posts. It was a peculiar feeling. I sensed I was itching to take
the kick. No, not because I had the possibility of putting my side
ahead, but because I was desperate by now to see if my technique
would work in a competitive environment. I was totally engrossed
with this technique and the routine which followed it. Everything
else, the conditions, the game and the crowd, was irrelevant. I got
my non-kicking foot in the exact position and when I struck the
ball it was sailing in the direction I intended. I was pleased that my
toes on my non-kicking foot were pointing in exactly the same
direction as when I started my run. It was immensely satisfying: I
could feel the right position to be in to kick the ball and if I had
any more kicks in this game I would use this technique. England
won the game 15–9, but I confess that I was perplexed by my
feelings afterwards. It did not dawn on me what the side had
achieved that day; all I could think about was my kicking technique
and how it worked. I was overjoyed and the significance of
this breakthrough overshadowed for me our win against the All
Blacks. However, the media and the world rugby population thought

otherwise and put that result down as one of England's finest victories.

It was a month or so before the first Five Nations game, against Scotland at Murrayfield. The English were licking their lips at the prospect of a try feast in the capital of Scotland. The Scots, on the other hand, were sharpening their claws, relishing the thought of putting one over on their old enemy. They certainly did not think they were there to make up the numbers. The hype and the pre-match build-up was about an England win and by how much. I can assure you, however, that the England team at no stage thought like that. They knew that the Scots would come out firing on all cylinders to put the record straight and that it would be a close one that day. The Friday before the game, Slem (Mike Slemen) and I sneaked on to the pitch for a bit of goal-kicking practice. Usually the home unions do not let you go on the grass unless you book a slot, but we went on with a couple of balls. It was just a case of finding the right positions and being familiar with the surroundings and picking up features which would help me line up the ball with the posts. I thought that, apart from a few penalties, I might have the opportunity to kick a few conversions in an international.

The game did not, however, go according to plan. We ran everything but just could not finish any of the moves. Panic crept in and we made a lot of mistakes. By half-time we were only being kept in contention by a solitary penalty goal. My success rate was a depressing one out of three and I was slightly concerned because, for the first time since adopting my technique, I did not feel confident. Something was wrong and if I was to kick my goals in the second half I had to sort it out – and sort it out quickly.

It was strange because I stumbled across my problem while Will Carling was addressing the team at half-time. I was crouched in the middle of the group, which is my customary position because, owing to a weak bladder, I have to relieve myself at half-time and I can scarcely leave the field of play. Will was bellowing orders at the rest of the players and asking everyone to look at him and concentrate. At this point I looked up and it dawned on me what I was doing wrong. I was lifting up my head too early. I was not focusing on the grass a metre in front of the ball. The eyes were left to wander without any purpose and raised too early – not dissimilar to a golfer lifting his head before he has hit the ball.

It was not long into the second half before I had the chance to see if the fault had been rectified. Very early on Will called for me to take a kick some 40 metres out. The feeling that I had experienced before my first kick against the All Blacks suddenly re-emerged. I was dying to take the kick, merely to reinforce my theory. Three times I had the opportunity to test it and three times the rhythm and strike produced points for the side. England were now leading 12 – 11 with a minute of normal time left to play. A victory seemed probable and all we had to do was to secure possession and belt the ball deep into the Scottish half. The line-out was lost, however, and all I could see was the ball going in slow motion to the outside-half, Gregor Townsend. He produced a dazzling drop goal that looked certain to upset the form guide and give Scotland a victory.

It was out-of-the-trenches time for England. We threw everything at the Scots at the restart because as long as the ball was in play we still had a chance of victory. There was a frantic passage when we attacked and the Scots counter-attacked. There was a pile-up and in the unbearable tension the referee awarded England a penalty. If kicked successfully a penalty would give England a one-point lead. From that moment my whole world became just one still picture. I knew Will would ask me to attempt the goal but at first I could not face it, I had to walk away. There were no particular thoughts in my head; everything seemed to be a blur. Will calmly called me over and said, 'Get on with it, it's easy.' Easy for him to say but he didn't have to do it. But this was what I had been selected for, to kick goals for England. It seemed a lifetime that I was there waiting to kick the ball, but never did a negative thought enter my head. What if I miss? I wonder what the time is? Will this be the last kick of the game? Will the game be lost on this kick? Nothing like that. I felt that I was totally alone, just out on the training pitch having a gentle knock-around with a few balls. I focused on getting the run-up right and making sure I got my kicking foot in the right position and made a good contact with the ball.

The crowd and the surroundings built up the tension which had been created from eighty minutes of frantic rugby. But I was oblivious of all this. I called the ball-boy on and he ran towards me with the kicking tee. He reached me and handed it to me with a gesture which was anything than offering me luck. I thanked him courteously because I felt that someone up above would smile upon me and give me a lucky strike when I needed it most. I placed the ball on the tee and got the line of the seam running straight through the middle of the post. Normally it takes me a couple of times to get this right and it is a question of fiddling with the ball until I am happy. My routine just happened. I did not give it a second thought. I was now in a position to approach the ball.

It was uncanny. There was this eerie silence. I was listening for the sound of the foot hitting the ball, hoping it would be a sweet 'pop'. Without thinking about anything else I started my run-up to the ball, leaned into it, sank my foot into it and struck it. The ball was on its way now, and there was nothing more I could do. For what seemed like hours I didn't look up but when – with some courage – I did, I could see the ball flying towards the right-hand post. I thought, no this can't be, it's going to hit the post. It's going to be all over. But the ball started to pull left towards the centre of the goal. It was going to go over. I still wasn't quite sure whether it had the legs to get there. I looked at the referee, he signalled that the goal was good, then immediately signalled the end of the game.

I knew then that all the hours of practice, all my good and bad experiences at Bath and the difficult games for England A and the South West had prepared me for this game and this moment. The experience was indescribable and to this day unforgettable, worth every minute of every hour of the preparation that made it possible. It proved to me that the despair associated with poor performances and the despondency that I felt after the Saracens game were a price worth paying for the high that I achieved when fulfilling my job well at an international level. It makes you want to do it again and again.

A Celebration of the Club Game

DAVID GREEN

Most of the contributors to this anthology have witnessed or played in any number of epic contests – Grand Slam deciders, Lions Tests and other such mighty battles from Brisbane to Bloemfontein, Durban to Dublin. But the international matches I have witnessed can be counted on the fingers of one hand. I have never been close to writing about one, never mind playing in one. Both as player and as rugby reporter my province has been the club scene, and this is less drab than it sounds. The game's pulse, it has always seemed to me, beats more strongly as one nears the grass roots. The aspects of high-profile matches can be distorted by media hype, costs of attendance for true lovers of the game pushed skywards, and availability of seats greatly reduced by the increasing influence of corporate hospitality. The clubs, which, after all, produce the players who grace the international scene, are bastions of sanity in a cock-eyed world.

As a boy, a small and weedy one prone to burst into tears at moments of crisis, I preferred the less obviously violent sports of cricket and soccer, though I always enjoyed watching rugby. My father, who played for Sale and Cheshire in the back row and might have gone further had business not dictated his removal to Paris for seven years from the age of twenty-one (poor man!), watched Sale regularly and I was happy to accompany him.

In the early and mid 1950s Sale were beginning to emerge from the trough that had followed the break-up of their fine pre-war side, which was studded with famous players. The great Welsh centre Claude Davey played as, for a time, did his international colleague, the formidable Wilfred Wooller. With England's Hal Sever on one wing and Ken Fyfe of Scotland on the other, Sale's backs must have put the wind up a few defences.

From around 1953, the time I started watching, Sale's results started to improve. Their captain was Tom Barker, a fine wing-forward who played in England trials and appeared regularly for Lancashire. Barker, whose career began as a prop at Northampton and ended as one at Sale, was almost equally at home on the blind-side as the open, and, though not particularly quick, had powerful ball-carrying skills to add to his formidable defence. I admired him greatly and, as a fifteen-year-old, would have found it impossible to credit that within four years I would be in the same team as him, listening avidly to his deep insights into the game and desperately trying to learn how to drink beer.

Sale had their fair share of big names in the 1950s. Bob Gemmill had been capped at lock by Scotland, who had also enlisted the services of Keith McMillan, a barrel-chested South African who, though built like a prop, played at number eight. Immensely strong, he was also a high-quality footballer. Sale's most famous player at that time, though, was Eric Evans, the hooker who won thirty caps between 1948 and 1958 and led England to the championship in 1957.

It is a characteristic of rugby union that men who would hardly be expected to perform impressively at any other sport can often find a niche within its framework where they can positively excel. Eric Evans was one of these. The gods had limited their gifts in his case to a certain wiry toughness but they had added, as counterbalance, an astonishing determination. He weighed barely twelve stone, he had no pace, his handling skills were limited. Undeterred, he trained and practised furiously, pestered more experienced players for advice and, by sheer grit, forced himself to the selectors' attention as a high-class hooker and a vigorous, spirited performer in the loose. Astonishingly, his first cap, against Australia, was at prop. His opposite number, Nick Shehadie, must have outweighed him by three and a half stones! Evans must have been well over forty by the time he finally retired in 1961. Right to the end nothing frightened him; he always sought the hottest part of the conflict.

Tom Barker had a good rugby brain, as did others, like McMillan, and Sale played some adventurous rugby. The use of failed penalty attempts as a springboard for attacking moves, usually begun by scissors or dummy scissors under one's own posts, is often credited to that great coach Carwyn James, who used the ploy regularly with Llanelli and the 1970 Lions. However, this was part of Sale's armoury years before, with Barker and McMillan doing the twiddly bit beneath the posts before the ball was moved wide to the faster men.

On one memorable occasion the attempt of the two burly back-row men to deceive the enemy ended in disaster, the cunning crossover resulting in the ball plopping miserably on to the turf. From my position on Sale's 25, I clearly heard Barker's aggrieved cry, 'What are you playing at, you silly bugger?' 'What are *you* playing at, man?' growled McMillan in reply. Red-faced glares were exchanged but a truce had been reached by the time the scrum had formed.

Sale had a pretty strong fixture list so I saw many well-known players from other clubs. At that time, when the County Championship was the main stepping-stone to an England trial and, possibly, subsequent glory, the strength of Yorkshire and Lancashire meant that northern clubs were major contributors to the England side. In addition, Sale played a quartet of Midland sides in Bedford, Coventry, Moseley and Northampton, who were all very strong, so much so that a rugby follower of thirty-five years ago would have been astonished that today none is numbered among England's top ten clubs.

I have clear memories of the dazzling half-back play of Gordon Rimmer of Waterloo and Martin Regan of Liverpool. They each got twelve caps but, although they were a fixture for years in the Lancashire side, England's selectors only played them together four times. Northampton were probably the best side in the country

145

until overtaken by Coventry around 1960. They had forwards of the calibre of Ron Jacobs and Don White, Dick Jeeps at scrum-half and an all-international three-quarter line in Frank Sykes, Jeff Butterfield, Louis Cannell and John Hyde. The packs these Midland clubs fielded regularly dwarfed our own, limiting our line-out possession and putting our scrum under pressure so as to slow and disrupt out-heel. In this lay the root of the insistence of Tom Barker, and of subsequent skippers, that any time the ball was kicked into our 25 the possibility of a counter-attack should be urgently considered. We didn't get all that much useful set ball, so when it was given to us, perhaps in a broken field, we should take advantage.

It was not until the early 1960s, following the arrival of Vic Harding, via Saracens and Cambridge, and the six foot ten Peter Stagg, whose capacity for socializing matched his height, that we had locks capable of winning quality line-out ball against class opposition.

From around nineteen years of age, I was playing 1st XV rugby during university vacations, and some of the distant, god-like figures of a few years before became boon companions. Looking back, we trained pretty hard, harder than most clubs, perhaps because we had in Freddie Griffiths, who played centre for Lancashire, Cheshire and the Barbarians, a fitness fanatic. Fred's qualification as a physiotherapist, a function he later fulfilled for Manchester City, was more than enough to fit him to oversee our preparations. However, we worked nothing like as hard as the top clubs do today. Thus, although up to 1965 the off-side laws made for limited space in midfield, scoring could be pretty high, since cover tended to get thinner and thinner as forwards tired.

The arrival of Stagg and Harding, together with that of the Old Millhillian Jim Roberts, who was to win sixteen caps on the left wing, made Sale capable of taking on the best sides while remaining capable of losing to moderate ones. In 1963 we beat Coventry, an almost unheard-of event, early in the season and went on to defeat the three other Midland sides. We were startled, as well as delighted, to defeat Coventry for they were immensely strong. Of their front row, two – Phil Judd and Herbie Godwin – were regular England players while the third – Mike McLean – was more feared than either. This trio were used by mothers in Coventry to frighten their offspring into obedience. Their locks, John Owen and Tom Pargetter, were current England players, like Judd and Godwin, and so was number eight Brian Wightman. The peerless Peter Robbins was at open-side. Behind they had goal-kicker supreme George Cole at scrum-half, with Tim Dalton, another England cap, at fly-half, and Peter Jackson on one wing and the equally dangerous Ricky Melville on the other. We felt as if we had turned over a Panzer division.

Our 16–6 triumph was the signal for some pretty serious celebrating, during which, at about 9 p.m., I spotted the Coventry front row sitting morosely in a dark corner of the main bar. I reeled across to them and said, 'Cheer up, lads, and come and have a gargle.' Judd shook his craggy head and said heavily, 'Well, if we can't beat bloody Sale . . .' and his voice trailed away into despairing silence. Despite his forebodings, Coventry had another outstanding year.

Peter Robbins was the best English openside of my time. A powerful, deep-chested man, he was quick over the ground, a heavy tackler with the ball skills of a top-quality centre. He also had an acute rugby brain, which constantly directed him into key areas of the field. He played opposing fly-halves like a skilful angler, enticing them with glimpses of a gap and then falling on them like a tower when they tried to go through it. An England regular from 1956, he lost his place to Budge Rogers in 1961. Despite Rogers's great energy and stamina and the dedication to fitness that underpinned his distinguished career he didn't, for us anyway, pose the same threat as Robbins, who was certainly unlucky to be discarded at the early age of twenty-eight.

If Robbins was unlucky then so – we at Sale thought – were our centre pair of Bill Patterson and Ken Nelson, both products of nearby Sale Grammar School and a feature of Sale and Cheshire sides from 1959 onwards. Patterson, tall, strong and long-striding, was a British Lion in New Zealand in 1959, two years before he gained his two England caps, a tally that scarcely reflected his quality as a player. Nelson, small but quick and elusive, was unluckier still, his nearest approach to recognition being a single England trial, in which he played out of position on the wing. It grieved us to see caps awarded to all sorts of blokes who had spots knocked off them whenever they encountered our two.

A move to Bristol, for reasons connected with cricket rather than rugby, severed my connection with Sale for a while, though it was renewed when I watched them in a journalistic capacity. It was Gloucestershire's offer of a cricket contract, following my dismissal by Lancashire at the end of the 1967 season, that dictated a move westwards. I had had some problems with a thigh muscle during the cricket season so my new employers were not keen for me to play rugby but they relented after I had negotiated the 1968 cricket season. By now rising twenty-nine I considered that my rugby-playing days were pretty well over but with my tendency to put on weight I had to do something to avoid turning up for nets in April looking like Orson Welles in the sherry advert. Bristol scrum-half Bill Redwood, whom I had known since we played cricket against each other at school, suggested I join Cleve, a local club with some testing fixtures, among them Gloucester United, Pontypool United and Cinderford over in the Forest of Dean. I took his advice and had three most enjoyable seasons.

Before the coming of leagues, rugby around Bristol was organized into what is still known as the Combination, an association of junior clubs who, while competing fiercely against each other, also acted as feeders to the Bristol club. This was not resented by the individual clubs, who were proud to have the quality of their young players recognized at a higher level. As compensation, when a Bristol player's career ended he would generally return to his Combination club and play on for a season or two, passing on what he had learned in the first-class scene. In Cleve's case, the then Bristol try-scoring record-holder Mike Ellery was still playing, as was ex-England hooker John Thorne. Although Ellery could only be persuaded to turn out for Cleve firsts in an injury crisis he was still very quick. Thorney was still hooking for the firsts, despite out-weighing each of his props by a good twenty pounds, and he would turn out, too, on a Sunday morning or any evening when it was light enough for thirty loonies to work up a thirst.

Combination players were regularly watched by Bristol's selec-tors, who were always on the look-out for new talent. Bristol were also happy for a XV selected from the Combination clubs to play an annual fixture on their Memorial Ground against the United side, which was the second team. Since the United would inevitably contain men with a good deal of first-team experience, this was a further opportunity to assess the potential of Combination players. It made for an effective system of progression for local players and provided Bristol with a steady flow of talent. To an extent this still happens, but the regulations over movement of players between clubs, essential if a league set-up is to function at all, tend to hamper the process.

Through playing for the Combination against the United I saw the Bristol club from closer quarters and was impressed. The ground, the stands, even the pitch itself, seemed vast compared with Northampton's and Coventry's, never mind Sale's, and there were many household names. I was flattered, therefore, when the chairman of selectors, Percy Redwood, who was Bill's father, asked me to take over the United captaincy for a couple of seasons. The reason for getting someone as elderly and varicose as me was that, if the United players, who were mostly youngsters, were to have any continuity it was important that their captain should not be competing for a first-team place. The previous year Mike Fry, later club skipper, had captained the United but had played half his games for the 1st XV. Clearly that was not going to happen to me. After some deliberation – I was not at all sure that at thirty-two I would be able to make an adequate contribution as a player and had no desire to be regarded as a passenger by the young pups – I accepted, beginning an association that was to continue for over a decade as I became, first, a tentative assistant coach, then a selector.

Bristol were organized differently from Sale. The latter, who were competing in the Manchester area with the likes of Wilmslow, Broughton Park and the Manchester club, ran five and sometimes six sides plus a Schools team, which played almost entirely in the holidays. Bristol, which had the back-up of the Combination clubs, limited themselves to two senior sides and a Colts XV. Because of this the concentration on training and the development of individual skills seemed to me more intensive, and the quality of rugby played, in the early 1970s anyway, to be higher. At that time Bristol were on a high. In 1971–2 they won unofficial club championships both for English clubs and for English–Welsh, that is, for those clubs from England and Wales which had enough fixtures across the Severn Bridge with each other to justify appearing in such a context.

They had internationals in the front row in Scottish prop Hamish Bryce and England's John Pullin. Mike Fry and Tony Rodgers were also top-class props and, with further England players in lock-forward Dave Watt, blindside David Rollitt and number eight Charlie Hannaford, their pack was seldom in any trouble. Indeed, with fine halves in Alan Pearn inside and skipper Tony Nicholls outside, Bristol could have limited themselves to a ten-man game and been very successful. However, they had some top-class backs too. They had three international wings in Alan Morley, Ken Plummer and Peter Knight, an excellent centre pairing in Jon Gabbitas and Chris Williams and, to paper over any cracks, David Tyler, who was a high-quality player at centre, wing or full-back. Most of the players remembered the dazzling football played during the seven or eight seasons from 1956 on, when the influence of John Blake at fly-half was paramount. During this period big, well-drilled forwards worked hard for possession, as they have always done, but once it was won Blake, partnered later by Redwood, launched attacks from all parts of the field, the most popular being their own 25, after which the emphasis was on continuity and support from all fifteen players.

Although errors and over-ambition inevitably led to some silly defeats, there were great victories, too. I can vouch for the problems this style of play gave opponents from a rare Sale visit to Bristol, who eventually won a lively game 19–14. After twelve minutes the Sale side was collectively knackered, having conceded two tries, chased the ball frantically all over the field without ever touching it except to restart. With such a tradition it was unlikely that Bristol would play stodgily, but there was more to the approach decided on by Nicholls and the coach, Peter Colston, a Blake-era player himself, than merely the desire to throw the ball around and have fun.

They agreed that unless all the skills a side possesses are called on, its full potential cannot be realized. Therefore, if limited tactics are employed, games will be lost that might have been won. They looked at the running potential of their squad and reasoned that if they could engineer enough broken fields to exploit, they would score enough tries to beat anyone. Broken fields are created in many ways, from one man beating another to the bringing of extra men into an attacking line to the gaining of swift loose ball when opposing defences are out of alignment. Colston and Nicholls also recognized, in agreement with the visionary Carwyn James, that, provided backs and forwards are alert and aware of their own required positional alignments, failed kicks, whether at touch or at goal, give many opportunities for launching attacks and, moreover, are presented rather than having to be worked for.

Refinements of these tactics included scissors and dummy-scissors runs designed to draw opponents to one area of the field so that the point of attack could be profitably switched to another. This sort of thing, built on the cornerstone of a big, mobile pack, produced much spectacular and effective rugby, the best contests being against London Welsh, then in their pomp and fielding a string of Lions and Welsh internationals, and against the big Welsh clubs who were naturally very strong during that decade of Welsh dominance. Even in midweek five-figure crowds turned up for the visits of Newport, Cardiff, Bridgend, Pontypool, Swansea or Llanelli. These fixtures, of course, had their death-knell with the formation of the leagues, and I believe much has been lost with their passing.

Bristol continued to produce successful sides under David Tyler, Mike Fry, Mike Rafter and Nigel Pomphrey. Tyler, of course, was happy to continue in the Colston–Nicholls pattern but the other three were forwards and naturally suspicious of dodgy-looking messing about with the ball deep in their own half. They neverthe- less each recognized the value of having a balanced side, of being able to attack the enemy on more than one front. Indeed, the back line of Mike Rafter's side, which defeated Leicester in the 1983 John Player Cup final – it read: Harding, Barnes; Carr, Knibbs, Hogg, Morley; Duggan – was fluent and inventive. Unfortunately, safety- first tactics set in in the later 1980s, leading to a gradual atrophy of the club's skill behind the scrum. A big, efficient pack keeps them comfortably in the first division, at least so far, but they no longer look likely to beat the best sides.

Looking back over nearly forty years as player and spectator there have been many changes, most of them for the better. When I started as a player the ball had to be played with the foot after a tackle before it could be picked up. At the line-out, centre- threequarters could, if they wanted, stand chest to chest in midfield, the line of off-side being the line of the line-out. Open-side wing forwards could detach from the scrum and advance towards the opposing fly-half on the line of the ball as it was heeled back through the opposing scrum. Changes to these laws, together with the Australian dispensation that prevents a player finding a direct touch (without bouncing) if he is outside his 22, created more space to play in, although recent alterations to laws relating to ruck and maul have, at least temporarily, removed most of it. The introduc- tion of leagues has brought benefits, not least the polarization of talent around a handful of clubs which makes the selectors' job a good deal easier. One must regret, though, the passing of the old-fashioned friendly matches, which weren't friendly at all until after the final whistle had blown.

One thing never alters and that is the friendliness of the club circuit, where virtually everyone is there because he or she loves the game and wishes to advance its interests. I write these words in May but already I am looking forward to the crisp Saturday afternoons of winter when the two sets of gladiators take each other on for eighty minutes and then an evening of camaraderie, discussion and reminiscence follows.

'For Neither Love Nor Money':
Modern Rugby Union and the
Victorian Concept of Amateurism

MARK BAILEY

More than either of its predecessors, the third Rugby World Cup has raised the profile of rugby union around the world. It has also proved another commercial success, generating income of millions of pounds from activities as diverse as sales of official merchandise, television rights and sponsors' packages. This, more than anything else, has served to underline the contradiction at the heart of rugby union: the modern game carries commercial weight across the globe, yet in principle it has remained strictly for amateurs. Rugby has been worthy of blue-chip sponsorship and prime-time television coverage for at least a decade, yet its stars have been officially denied any direct financial reward for their skills and dedication. Little wonder, then, that World Cup year has concentrated minds on the great 'amateurism debate'.

To a casual follower of sport, the endless debates during the summer of 1995 on amateurism in rugby union must have appeared perverse, anachronistic and – at times – downright confusing. For example, our casual follower might begin by wondering why rugby authorities throughout the world have for so long opposed the payment of such high-profile, international sportsmen. The answer to his question is that many of the people running rugby are committed to maintaining the game as an amateur pastime. In which case, muses our observer, why did the authorities dilute the amateur principle by allowing players to receive some remuneration and material preferment for a range of off-the-field activities and pro-motional work? Er, because such work is 'non-rugby-related' and subject to various controls and regulations. But how can one prop-erly distinguish between activities which are rugby-related and non-rugby-related? Why was no action taken on reports that French and South African players receive direct cash payments? How did Mike Catt escape punishment after admitting to receiving £200 'fixed expenses' when playing in South Africa, while Adrian Spencer of Cambridge University was banned for playing alongside rugby league professionals as an unpaid amateur? Er, no comment.

The World Cup has cast in a stark and unattractive light the doomed attempts of rugby union's authorities to embrace simul-taneously the rewards of big-business and the ethos of amateurism. It is no coincidence that the International Rugby Football Board (IRFB) chose World Cup year finally to confront the contradictions and confusions within the game. In March 1995 Vernon Pugh admitted that 'we, the administrators, have brought about the pre-sent state of affairs. We demand the commitment, success, money, prestige, time and much more of the lives of others whose interests we should have learned to be more respectful of, and yet we seek to deny the reward and compensation that many would expect to represent the equitable balance.' Here, at last, was an explicit acceptance that the rugby authorities could not in all conscience occupy the moral high ground on amateurism, when they alone were responsible for intensifying the demands of players and creat-ing the clamour for payment.

There is no doubt that the regulations relating to amateurism were unworkably complex and arcane, and for many years the IRFB itself had been either reluctant or unable to police them consistently around the world. Rugby union was rightly derided of its 'shamat-eurism', and the game needed sanitizing. Even so, the International Board's decision at its Paris meeting in August 1995 to repeal all the regulations relating to amateurism was astonishingly far-reaching and audacious.

No one in the rugby world denies that the sudden repeal of the amateur regulations will create many new problems: is there enough money in the game to pay even the leading players? What of administrators and referees? Will a system of transfer fees for players be introduced, and will the issue of player-qualification for provincial and national sides become contentious? How will professionalism affect relations with rugby league? Doubtless these and many other issues will be addressed in due course. But for all the commotion in the media about the IRFB's new stance on professionalism, one important issue has been overlooked: the status of amateurism. It is supremely ironical that the introduction of professionalism has *failed* to resolve the question of amateurism in rugby union. Individual unions can still decide whether they wish to embrace or reject professionalism, because the IRFB's decision is permissive and not mandatory. While New Zealand and South Africa have embraced the brave new world with ill-concealed glee, there are still many real and potential dissenters. A genuine dislike of professional rugby remains deep-rooted in the upper echelons of the game in Argentina, Ireland and England. And, most astonishing of all, the French authorities have recently announced their intention to reject professionalism in order to preserve rugby union's special qualities and spirit.

A cynic might argue that the French response was influenced more by the potential loss of government funding for professionalized rugby than a commitment to rugby's amateur ethos. But France has always espoused rugby union's special qualities, and there is a real fear that full-blown professionalism will destroy those qualities. Other nations have been slower to respond officially to the IRFB's announcement, although the French have merely articulated the concerns of rugby people everywhere: could rugby retain its distinctive ethos if it turned professional? This is an issue of fundamental importance, and one which has received remarkably little attention within the game. The media attention has tended to focus upon the stubborn adherence of rugby's administrators to amateurism, the hypocrisy of the old regulations and the defensive reactions of administrators to such criticism. Far too little effort has been devoted to exploring or explaining *why* the basic tenets of amateurism are worth preserving. The IRFB has now forced rugby union to face these issues, to think very carefully about the type of game it wants for the future, and to implement that vision at national level.

This essay offers no solutions to rugby's pressing problems. Its objective is modest, and seeks merely to consider one vital issue that has been notable by its absence from recent debates: the concept of amateurism itself. 'Amateurism' is sacred to rugby's administrators, but what exactly does it stand for? Why is the amateur ethos held with such reverence and fervour by the game's administrators? What qualities does amateurism bring to the game, and – crucially – would the character of the game be changed if we abandoned it?

The concept of amateurism can only be understood properly by placing it within the broader context of the evolution of sports and recreation in nineteenth-century Britain. Around 1800, most communities participated in a wide variety of traditional games and leisure activities. Historically, the British have exhibited a particular affection for recreational pursuits, and a flair for creating new forms and variants. These traditional recreations did not survive the profound economic, social and cultural changes of the nineteenth century, either disappearing entirely or evolving into more organized sports. Victorian Britain marked a crucial stage in the transition from 'crude', 'irregular' and 'unrefined' games to those which were regarded as 'organized', 'disciplined', 'refined' and 'rational'. Many complex factors combined to bring about this metamorphosis, but the emergence of standardized team sports from a corpus of traditional games was particularly influenced by the rise of secondary education. It is no coincidence that the public schools were the driving forces behind the establishment of the Football Association (1863), the Rugby Football Union (RFU) (1871), and the Amateur Athletics Association (1881).

The enthusiasm with which the public schools embraced standardized team sports was partly due to the propaganda that extolled the virtues of such activities. In keeping with the Victorian obsession with 'rationality', sport had to fulfil some logical and justifiable purpose. It was distinct from work, but it was not to be regarded as some uncontrolled and idle pastime. Sport should provide not only physical exercise, but also inculcate acceptable ideals and rational purposes into its participants. Paramount among these was the ethic of communal effort and the subjugation of the individual for the common good, a model of behaviour which would be beneficial to both individual and country. Rational sport was founded upon self-discipline, orderliness, sobriety, restraint and respectability. In other words, it was a means to social improvement, and as such it offered a potential solution to contemporary concerns about the social ills of urbanization and the potential disorder among the lower orders of society.

Thus, to the Victorians, team sports were as much about a social philosophy as about physical exercise. They provided moral and physical health in a sedentary middle class, together with rational, disciplined recreation for a rational, disciplined workforce. It proved a potent combination, because the success and popularity of team sports in late-Victorian Britain was remarkable. By the last quarter of the nineteenth century, many of these team sports had firmly established themselves across the social scale. Yet it was the very popularity of organized sport that generated growing pressure for the payment of its leading protagonists. In the 1880s and 1890s, the administrators of football, cricket and rugby union were all forced to address the issue of professionalism directly. Of these, only rugby union refused to accept the principle of payment for playing, thus precipitating the famous split with the northern clubs in 1893.

By the 1890s the distinction between amateurs and professionals was clearly a contentious issue among rugby's administrators, but why did rugby not reach a compromise in the manner of football and cricket? What was so unpalatable about professionalism, and what was so important about amateurism?

An explanation is not hard to find, and it carries important implications for the modern debate. As we have seen, team sport embodied a social philosophy of the *way* to play the game, involving moral virtues of self-discipline, 'fair' competition, and the 'proper' style of play. The process of playing meant everything, and the outcome of playing meant nothing. Sport was founded upon a spirit of participation and commensality, and therefore possessed a fundamentally different ethos from work where behaviour was dictated by success and profits. If sport became a profession, then it would automatically lose both its distinctiveness and its intrinsic values. Professionals who depended upon winning for their livelihood would inevitably reject the all-embracing but unwritten spirit and etiquette of the game, with its sense of fair play and the joy of participation. The pursuit of victory as an end in itself would destroy self-discipline, restraint and responsibility.

By definition, the professionalization of sport would involve the acquisition of business principles and modes of behaviour. In doing so, professional sport would lose the distinctive and rational basis of amateur sport, and with it the purpose and prospects of social improvement. These concerns were especially pertinent to rugby, a game founded upon remorseless, aggressive physical contact and governed by complex laws. The nature of rugby demanded restraint and self-discipline among its participants at all times, and therefore could not be trusted to professional players.

To what extent is this concept of amateurism prevalent among rugby union administrators of the 1990s? If we are to believe some of the more extreme caricatures painted in the media, their adherence to this principle has not wavered for a century. For example, a recent commentary in *Time Out* magazine characterized the English RFU as populated by 'true-blue amateurs', vainly attempting to preserve 'the game on what could be termed socialistic lines': the author of the article could scarcely suppress his incredulity at the continued presence of what he regarded as 'a cherished amateur ethos'.

There are some grounds for arguing that the RFU deserves such facile stereotyping of its views. Its stance on amateurism has been staunchly conservative, and its officers have regularly and vocally affirmed their commitment to the amateur principle. However, the actions of the RFU in the 1990s would be anathema to the 'true-blue amateurs' of the 1890s. The modern RFU needs a 'competitions sub-committee' to co-ordinate the various league and cup competitions among its member clubs, but the very act of competing in leagues (or in a World Cup) is wholly incompatible with the spirit of Victorian amateurism. By definition, a competitive structure places emphasis on results rather than participation, and the Victorians would argue that this inevitably destroys both the restraint and rational purpose which constitute the *raison d'être* of amateur sport. Indeed, one of the issues that divided the northern clubs from the rugby union in the 1890s was the desire to organize league rugby.

Similarly, the modern RFU's attitude to the preparation and success of the England team would have been wholly unacceptable to the RFU of the 1950s. A turning point might have been reached in the early 1960s, when a president of the RFU entered the England dressing room at the Arms Park and informed the team that defeat against Wales by four tries to three was infinitely preferable to victory in a dour penalty shoot-out. Once the presidential party had left the room, an apoplectic chairman of selectors told the team that they should be bloody well delighted with a 3–0 win. This anecdote encapsulates perfectly the clash between the true amateur ethos and the modern thirst for success. Further examples of this changing attitude are apparent off the field. For instance, an institution which has deftly courted commercial sponsorship to rebuild its ground at Twickenham, and which has rowed publicly with Oxbridge over the financial spoils of the Varsity Match, can scarcely be either 'true-blue amateur' or committed to running rugby along 'socialistic lines'. The recent activities and actions of the RFU, if not always its words, are some distance removed from the world of 'noble and cherished' amateurism.

The split with rugby league in the 1890s inevitably cast rugby union as the leading defender of the Victorian concept of amateurism, a role and position that is still accepted by some within the game today. But in reality this is an empty stance, for even the conservative RFU has failed to live up to amateurism's exacting principles for many years. Consequently, those administrators who have clung blindly to the amateurism principle must accept public condemnation and derision for their empty rhetoric and self-delusion, and for their failure to redefine what 'amateurism' now represents.

The failure of rugby union to defend and uphold the Victorian concept of amateurism cannot, however, be blamed upon its administrators. Victorian amateurism has failed for the simple reason that the concept itself was too deeply flawed to be tenable. As we have seen, the Victorians believed that the primary function of sport was to act as a medium of social improvement, but that its social benefit and purpose would be destroyed by the receipt of material benefit.

This is a powerful ethos, but it possesses two obvious weaknesses. First, the assumption that sport can successfully impart strong moral values and purity of purpose in its participants is an admirable ideal, but for many people an unattainable goal. Creating a moral code is one thing; persuading the majority to adhere to it is another. Sport has certainly become a religion, but not in the manner envisaged by Victorian zealots. Second, the logic of the concept of amateurism is too rigid and absolute. It is certainly reasonable to suppose that professionalism will change a participant's approach to sport, and dilute his commitment to self-improvement and moral advancement: but this does not necessarily imply that professionalism will eradicate all sense of moral value and self-improvement. Implicit in the Victorians' logic is the assumption that the amateur is a gentleman of impeccable behaviour, while the professional is an inveterate cheat and a cad to boot. David Gower, Jack Nicklaus and Gary Lineker are living proof that professionalism does not destroy dignity, self-discipline, responsibility and the sense of how to play the game. And even if the Victorians' logic was tenable, a desire to win at all costs is scarcely high on the list of immoral and unacceptable behaviour.

The obvious conclusions of this discussion are scarcely new or original: that Victorian amateurism was an unrealistic ideal, and that rugby union has been falling short of its demands for decades. However, the implication which flows from them is rather more disconcerting, namely that amateurism is not an issue in the game. It might have been a relevant and live issue for debate in the 1950s and 1960s, but no longer. And if amateurism is no longer an issue in rugby union, then it follows that neither is professionalism.

When administrators talk about the need to defend amateurism in rugby, they are actually using the term 'amateurism' as a euphemism for those distinctive qualities which make rugby union so attractive to players, administrators and spectators alike. Of course, such qualities are difficult to define, which explains the readiness to resort to a label such as 'amateurism'. But rugby union does possess a distinctive spirit, an undeniable 'feel-good' factor. Its attractiveness lies in its social diversity, its camaraderie, and its non-vocational nature. Its fundamental principle – that the game embodies a commitment to contribution, not extraction – strikes a sympathetic chord in a Christian and caring society. Furthermore, rugby provides a test of physical prowess for people possessing a variety of physical shapes and sizes, yet who are bonded together by a spirit of self-control and mutual respect. The concept of 'amateurism', and the Victorian spirit of how to play the game, have contributed significantly to the creation and shaping of these attributes, although it does not follow that the payment of a few players will inevitably undermine them.

So when the rugby authorities talk of the need to preserve 'amateurism', in reality they are referring to the need to preserve the game's 'special qualities'. The two concepts are linked, but they are also discrete entities. Also, their sense that those special qualities have been eroded in recent years, and remain seriously threatened by changes in the modern game, are well founded.

There is little doubt that the majority of people within rugby would applaud and support the efforts of their ruling bodies to protect those 'special qualities'. The prospect of following the same route of other major sports, where such qualities are scarcely evident, remains the recurrent nightmare of rugby's administrators. Football at the highest level is controlled by money, and the FA have little effective power to tackle the numerous problems that fester within the game: violence, over-playing, and allegations of corruption and match-rigging. English county cricket cannot release itself from the grip of commercial interests to reorganize the game in the best interests of the national team. In athletics, independent agents have lined their pockets and those of the top performers, while the grass roots remained strapped for cash. And the Australian Rugby League has been embroiled in a costly and damaging court battle with Rupert Murdoch over the creation of a club super-league. Is this the future for rugby union?

Such depressing examples are employed by many people within rugby union to paint a harrowing picture of the reality of professional sport. The professionalization of rugby union, they argue, would lead to similar problems. But the argument that professionalism is the main threat misses the point. Excessive commercialism, not professionalism, is the greatest threat to rugby union's distinctive qualities. And the threat is all the greater because commercial sponsors are attracted to rugby's special qualities. Professionalism is merely the consequence of commercialism. Thrown back on their own resources (such as subscriptions, bar-takings, attendance money, and fund-raising activities), few – if any – rugby clubs in Britain could afford to pay their players. Consequently, professionalism is only feasible through the financial backing of sponsors, and many clubs would even struggle to support a professional staff *with* outside sponsorship. Remove commercialism, and you remove the financial basis of professionalism.

Over-commercialization of sport carries four adverse consequences. First, commercialism changes sporting attitudes more rapidly than any other factor, because commercialism chases winners. The more that success on the field equates with financial reward and material preferment, the more individual players, clubs and unions will place the pursuit of success above all other considerations. Second, with commercialism as the driving force, financial rewards will not be distributed evenly throughout the game, and the ensuing imbalance will undoubtedly destabilize it. Indeed, it is precisely those who have been empowered by commercialism, such as the leading players and the senior clubs/provinces, who pose the greatest threat to the rugby authorities. Third, commercialism carries obligations to the sponsor, and the sponsor's objectives are likely to be different from those of the game and its traditions. The essence of rugby union is that each player has an obligation to his opponents, to his team-mates and to the game; the essence of commercialism is that obligations exist only between the financial donor and recipient. And lastly, commercialism demands exposure in return for its investment. Eventually, the power of commercialism will dominate decision-making in the sport, demanding more fixtures and more competitions. The consequence will be over-exposure at the top level, both in terms of time and money, which reduces interest in and the standards of the sport.

This discussion has deliberately highlighted the adverse consequences of over-commercialism. But this is not to argue that rugby should eschew all commercial links. Rugby union, like all sports, needs money to nurture its grass roots. Development of the game among the young and the disadvantaged requires financial support, and this can be achieved effectively only through sponsorship. Rugby union needs commercial sponsorship, but it must be clear-sighted and selective in its choice of sponsors and the nature of the obligations that a commercial contract brings.

If the rugby authorities wish to control the game, they must take firm steps to control the spread of commercialism. Excessive commercialism knows the price of everything and the value of nothing, and will destroy rugby's special qualities. The danger for any sport comes when the influence of commercial forces reaches a critical mass, and rugby union is fast approaching that point. This is the vital issue which needs to be addressed, and with immediate effect. Few – if any – administrators in rugby have publicly debated the adverse consequences of commercialism: few have articulated a vision of what rugby union *could* be like in future, and what it *should* be like. The rugby authorities will have a much stronger case with which to resist 'professionalism' when they develop and articulate a clear sense of what rugby stands for after 'amateurism'.

Rugby is suffering from an acute identity crisis, of which the debate on amateurism is only a symptom. Commercialism threatens the game's identity, yet the administrators continue to embrace it with seemingly little thought for its consequences. Indeed, the players, the media, the public and the rugby authorities seem to have distracted themselves with the side-show of 'amateurism'. Yet only when the authorities temper and control their own thirst for commercialism can they realistically hope to quench the players' thirst for money. A failure to recognize this soon will have far-reaching consequences, for rugby will lose its noble qualities and allow the baser human desires for money and success to prevail.

The Year We Got It Right

ROGER UTTLEY

It is fourteen years since I last had the pleasure of donning the white shirt of England. In that short space of time a lot has happened to me. I am certainly older, not necessarily wiser and like most high achievers in sport am no longer able to attain the high standards that, with the ignorance of youth, one rather took for granted. Whilst not regretting my lot, I cannot but envy the ability of, say, musicians, who can maintain their productive peak for much longer.

Looking back at my own career during the 1970s, England's most productive decade ever, there were many peaks and troughs. The Welsh and French teams of the same period were extremely competitive and stuffed full of *hwyl*, Gallic flair, and, from an Englishman's viewpoint, a very unfair distribution of talent in the form of such illustrious players as J.P.R. and J.J. Williams, Gerald Davies, Gareth Edwards, Phil Bennett, Mervyn Davies, Walter Spanghero, Jo Maso, Jean-Pierre Lux, Jean-Claude Skrela, Jean-Pierre Rives and Jean-Pierre Bastiat. The list could continue, and it really was very unfair. Add to this the perennial problem of the selection system in England (at the time) and one can begin to see the sort of problem we faced as players during this period.

There was plenty of experience available and no shortage of talented players. Unfortunately lack of consistency, allied to a complete lack of a corporate plan that might allow the national side to draw on the large resources of players available at club level in England, meant that time and again the national side was thwarted in its repeated attempts to win a Five Nations Championship and

166

Grand Slam. In 1977, my first season as captain, we got off to a flying start against Scotland in the Calcutta Cup at Twickenham, winning by 26 points to 6. We squeaked through against Ireland in Dublin by 4 points to 0 and then, despite pressurizing France for huge chunks of the game at Twickenham, were not able to translate this into points on the board and went down by a solitary point, 3 points to 4 – which was galling, though not nearly as bad as losing 9–14 to Wales at Cardiff in the last match of the season.

That match in particular was a nightmare. It was England's worst performance of the season and Wales's best, both by some margin. Places were up for grabs for the Lions tour to New Zealand and so was the captaincy. The net result was that Phil Bennett got the captaincy and Wales got the highest representation of one of the home unions on any Lions tour. To make matters worse, I picked up an injury (a not uncommon occurrence at this stage of my career). This finally manifested itself as the tour party met in London immediately prior to departure. After the first training session I found it difficult to sit with any degree of comfort. The result was that as the team flew out to Auckland I made my weary way back to Newcastle suffering from a prolapsed disc and the very real prospect of never playing again.

During this period I nearly packed it all in. Back pain can be debilitating at the best of times but to someone used to exercising at will it was a severe blow. Various treatments and a lot of hard work ploughing up and down a variety of swimming pools and working out in gyms gradually brought me back to fitness. Within nineteen months of sustaining the injury I was back in an England shirt. In my first match we lost to New Zealand at Twickenham. I was even re-appointed as captain against Scotland in the opening match of the 1979 championship, a game we should have won instead of courteously allowing Scotland to earn a draw. The next match was in Dublin and I must have become the first player to have been picked, not only to play but to lead the team, to suffer a temperature of 102 degrees on the Friday evening, withdraw from the match on the Saturday and then get dropped for the following match without ever having played – talk about inconsistent selection!

These events coincided with a major career shift for me during the summer of 1979. A new job which gave me more time to train and the prospect of new challenges on the field with my new club, Wasps, meant I had plenty to keep me interested. My northern links were kept open with appearances for Northumberland in the County Championship at the start of the 1980 season. A good run with them meant selection for the North squad that was due to play the All Blacks at Otley in November. Things really seemed to be looking up. I felt fitter than I had done for ages. To be able to move in a pain-free, unrestricted manner was tremendously liberating. My confidence came oozing back and I actually looked forward to the physical confrontation of the game against the All Blacks, which I hoped would prove I still had something to offer at the top level.

Selection for the North meant a lot. The likes of Tony Neary, Peter Dixon, Fran Cotton, Steve Smith, Alan Old and myself had all suffered varying degrees of hurt during the 1970s in our various bids to play for England. Now, when it was almost too late we were being given another opportunity to tilt at the big boys, albeit in the red shirts of the North. Several other things made this match special. One was the calm and confidence I felt in the changing room before going out. Another was the atmosphere in the tiny ground at Otley: with spectators sitting in the poplar trees at one end of the ground, it was electric. The match itself showed just what a common-sense selection of Englishmen could produce against an All Blacks Test side. We beat them 21 points to 9, with Alan Old going over for the final try and converting it to seal our triumph. The reaction afterwards was fantastic and gave English rugby a much-needed shot in the arm, with many knowledgeable people talking of the game as one of the great performances outside an international match. The only sad part of that day was that Peter Dixon announced his retirement from rugby after the match.

Those of us in the England squad then travelled down to Leicester for a training session and the announcement of the England side to play the All Blacks at Twickenham the following week. All they had to do, surely, was to pick the North side in its entirety – a bold choice, perhaps, but not without its merits – or so we smugly thought as we travelled down the M1 after the match.

The following morning was bright and sunny. But it wasn't the way I was feeling. For the first time in my international career I had been asked to sit on the bench. Apparently my jaw hit the floor when Mike Rafter's name was read out rather than my own by Budge Rogers, the chairman of selectors. I now had to try to give the selected XV as much support as possible while believing that I should be out there on the field myself. It was certainly good for character-building, and I felt a lot for the likes of John Olver and Dewi Morris who spent their fair share of time on the bench during my term as coach with England in the late 1980s.

That particular XV were not up to the job, a galvanized All Black side hitting them on the rebound to win by a single point. With another championship looming everything was up for grabs once again. The final trial was held over the Christmas holiday period and whilst the match followed its less than useful course, it did allow Phil Blakeway, the Gloucester tight-head prop, to re-emerge after an inauspicious debut on the 1975 Australian tour. His selection was critical to my chances. His scrummaging power meant that the England front five could take on most opposition packs on their own. This left room for my selection on the blindside. Not being the quickest thing on two legs it allowed me the choice of standing off on the short side on the opposition's put-in. It appeared that, like the players, the national selectors had been learning a few harsh lessons over recent years.

Under the direction of coach Mike Davis, England were for once able to capitalize on the vast experience available to them. With four former captains in the pack, Bill Beaumont had an easy ride motivating a side that had flair and pace in the back line, plus the tremendous bonus of Dusty Hare place-kicking at full back. As with preparation for the North v. New Zealand match before Christmas, things felt right as soon as the team for the opening match against Ireland was announced.

After a magnificent tour of Australia the previous summer, Ireland were not only favourites to beat us, but stood a good chance – according to popular opinion – of winning the championship. They had won both Tests in Australia, and what was even more remarkable, they did it after dispensing with the services of Tony Ward, who had scored a record thirty-eight points in the 1978 campaign. He had been hailed as Ireland's new saviour, but a young man by the name of Ollie Campbell was to appear on the scene and steal the glory in Australia.

The men in green were hot favourites. That suited us just fine. There was a quiet but determined mood in the side as England took the field for that 1980 International Championship match. Our plan was to dominate up front, because that was where our strength lay. By using the principles of the North's win over the All Blacks, we were going to get amongst them, apply maximum pressure and get as many points on the board as possible. We established that forward domination, but found ourselves 3 points to 9 down after twenty minutes, with Ollie Campbell in great kicking form. The pattern was familiar; surely we weren't on that same old road to ruin again. Our equalizing score came when, after pressing near their line, we tied up the Irish defence and Steve Smith had the simplest of tasks – to pick up the ball and dive over. Steve was also the instigator of the try that took us in front just before the interval. With his way ahead blocked, Steve kicked through to the Irish corner. Mike Slemen went round Kevin O'Brien, who had played for the North at Otley and was now winning his first cap for Ireland, but he was being shown very little consideration by his Lancashire colleagues on this day.

Dusty duly converted both these tries and we turned round 15 points to 9 in front. With our control so complete, Ireland never had a look-in during the second half. Dusty kicked his second penalty before John Scott picked up from a scrum and ran 15 yards for a try, which he acknowledged by holding the ball aloft in a one-armed salute. The only setback we suffered that day was when Tony Bond broke his leg after an hour and was replaced by Clive Woodward, making his debut. Everyone was delighted with the 24–9 result – as many points as the side had scored in the whole of the previous championship – and with our performance. We won so much good ball and kept such tight control that we destroyed a side which had been highly rated. When you consider the way Ireland were to thrash the Welsh at the end of the season, it made a nonsense of their display against us. They were better than the result indicated, but they were not allowed to be. That's how we played it that season – with control, not allowing the opposition to play the rugby they wanted. Alas, like the night of our win over Scotland four years previously, the evening celebration was spoilt by an action of incredible thoughtlessness, even by the standards of the England selectors. Nigel Horton had come into the side when injury forced out Maurice Colclough. At the time he was living in France. The Midlands lock put in a solid performance and fitted in so well that our effectiveness was not reduced at all. With a long way still to go, he would have been useful to have around. We all guessed that Maurice might regain his place; but tomorrow was another day.

After the dinner was finished and we were getting ready for the dance, I came across a very distressed Kay Horton. I asked what the trouble was and she said that Nigel had just been told he wasn't playing in the next game. 'You're joking,' I exclaimed. It was obvious she was not. I went to find Nigel and asked him what had happened. He was in a terrible state: totally distraught and actually crying. He said that this was the finish as far as he was concerned: he didn't want to know any more.

Fancy telling anybody that his services wouldn't be required the night after he had played his guts out for his country! Budge was very lucky not to get planted by Nigel, who in any case must have known in his own heart that Maurice was likely to come back. Anything, though, can happen with injuries and loss of form and you would think the selectors would want to keep as many options open as possible. It was distressing to watch his humiliation.

A lot of the young players didn't appreciate what was going on, but the senior lads were disappointed with what had happened. England's magnificent man-management again! It was almost as if they were trying to think how best to destroy the tremendous team spirit we had created that afternoon. The whole affair cast a gloomy shadow over the celebrations which was all the more devastating because the distress was totally unnecessary. Maurice did come back for our game in Paris, and was the only change from the side that had finished the game against Ireland. Poor Tony Bond would be out for the season and Clive retained his place.

Paris was certainly not a happy hunting ground for England; they had last won there in 1964 and had never been victorious at the Parc des Princes. Training in the damp in Paris and then Versailles we gained even more confidence because the weather was ideal for us. Instead of sharing with Tony Neary, I was stuck with John Scott – from beauty to the beast, you may say. As a precaution I slept with the mattress on the floor to give a more solid base for my back. But my nightmare of further disc trouble became a reality when I woke early in the morning to find that after two days' training and travelling my back had seized up again. John Scott was oblivious to the world as I dragged myself off the floor. It was about half-past six and there was no one about. It had always been my big fear that I would have to cry off on the morning of a big game like this.

I needed to get heat on my back so I went into the shower; there I was hobbling around in there, like Corporal Jones from *Dad's Army*, thinking, don't panic, don't panic. I leaned on the wall with one arm so that the hot water sprayed the affected area and after about half an hour, the pain began to ease. I felt fit enough to move around, so I went to see Don Gatherer. Don opened the door rather bleary-eyed, but soon had his magic fingers working their miracles and I became one of the England team again.

The journey to the ground by motorcade was as exciting as ever, and Steve Smith and I sat at the front enjoying the view of the four gendarmes on motorbikes carving out a path for us. If any cars are too slow to get out of the way, the French police are not frightened to deposit a large boot into the side-panel of the offending vehicles. This got us in the right mood for the battle ahead. By the time we had our photograph taken, the rain had stopped, but it was still overcast. The going was heavy, which suited our strong pack perfectly.

As you leave the changing room, you can get a view of the proceedings through the large glass doors. As we came out for the last time, the sun was streaming through the glass and I turned to Tony and said, 'Bloody hell!' The French with the sun on their backs are a dangerous lot; the warm atmosphere seems to fill them all with that traditional Gallic flair and daring. Just to prove the point, their captain, Jean-Pierre Rives, rounded off a thrilling movement to score a try in the opening minute. Seconds later we were back at the half-way line as though the game was about to start all over again; unfortunately, we were four points adrift and had plenty to make up.

That was just the sort of opening that had heralded several humiliating English defeats at French hands in recent years. To be behind our own line without having even broken into a sweat was a demoralizing feeling. Yet we were determined that this was not the beginning of another French avalanche. We'd been behind against the Irish and worked our way back; although we had made it difficult for ourselves, this was what we had to do again. And, with our pack in outstanding form, we slowly hauled ourselves back.

John Carleton and Nick Preston could not have timed their first tries for England any better, and John Horton dropped goals either side of the interval to take England in front by 17–7. I missed both these kicks because I was off the field receiving treatment. Jean-Luc Joinel had tapped me behind the ear with his boot and I once again left the field with blood streaming down. In the medical room Mike Davis was getting very agitated, for the officials were asking irrelevant questions like the address of my doctor back home. I don't know whether this useless information was supposed to delay my return to the action, but luckily Doctor Leo Walkden came in and stitched me up. He said that I'd had a lucky escape as Joinel's kick had just missed the cerebral artery.

All I wanted to do was to get back and I was delighted to find that our lead had increased from a slender 10–7 into 17–7, courtesy of John Horton. That the side had raised their game because they were one short demonstrated why the 1980 side was different. Our scrum had been giving the French a terrible pasting, but, as the game went on, and Phil Blakeway suffered from a rib injury, their forwards at last responded to the cheers of the French supporters. We faced a torrid time in the final minutes. When the French cut loose, then you're in big trouble . . . and we played right into their hands by missing touch several times and allowing them back into the action. From one of those breaks, Averous went over. Our plight was not helped when Caussade converted from the touchline. But, after a traumatic finale, we just stayed ahead to register England's first win in Paris for sixteen years.

The French had fought us every inch of the way and the game had been played at a tremendous pace; we all slumped exhausted in the dressing room, but the euphoria of winning made up for any physical tiredness. The only thing that annoyed us was that we had had the French on the rack and allowed them back into the game. We could sort that out later.

Evenings in Paris are always memorable, especially when you've also enjoyed the rare taste of victory. The dinner disintegrated into chaos when, after we had been presented with after-shave and records, John Scott, I think it was, discovered that the records made impressive frisbees. If you didn't have your head knocked off by one of them, then a soaking in after-shave would follow. The French police were also very protective, staying with us to enjoy the fun for most of the evening. I went to bed reasonably early because of my headache, but the action continued well into the night. Clive Woodward had a beautiful velvet jacket destroyed and the following morning Steve Smith had more trouble with re-entry than any of the Apollo spaceships.

That victory rather unexpectedly opened up all sorts of opportunities, not least the chance of the Grand Slam. At that point we led the table with two wins out of two, Ireland, Scotland and France all having lost at least once. Our next game, against the only other unbeaten side – Wales – was the crunch and would decide whether this England team was different after all or just another side full of false promises.

The importance of this game dawned on us as the media proceeded to give the confrontation a significance which a rugby game simply does not merit. Labelled the 'match of the decade' (which wasn't difficult as we were only six weeks into the eighties), this battle drew its ingredients from a variety of sources. Six years had passed since England had last beaten Wales; even then the Welsh had complained about some 'blind Irish referee', and had refused to allow us even the smallest crumb of credit for our success. Wales were now on the decline; this was obvious to everybody. However low the Welsh fall, though, the one thing their supporters refuse to contemplate is losing to England. Now questions were being asked about whether their team would have the ability to cope with an England side with two wins under their belt. The English rugby press, so used to national disasters, had begun to build us up as the greatest thing since sliced bread and kept enthusing over our qualities.

Everything that could be thrown in the melting pot was. The papers alleged that Fran Cotton had called Graham Price a cheat for always taking the scrum down, and was going to sort him out. John Scott, too, was playing against three of his Cardiff colleagues and was going to take them on. You could not pick up a paper without some new revelation about the England–Wales contest.

Everybody was making something out of the match, which we as international players accepted as the norm. The man of the moment was Paul Ringer of Wales. It is his name that will live longest in the memories of this match, but even before he took the field, he was earmarked as the man most likely to cause trouble. His performance against France a month earlier had later been analysed by television commentators: while he may have fooled the referee that day, his crimes could not get by the slow-motion camera and many felt that he should not have been chosen. What Paul Ringer felt about all this press coverage, I don't know, but that afternoon at Twickenham he played like a man who totally believed in his own publicity.

Inevitably, all the press baiting found its way into the minds of the players; it was impossible not to let the pressure get to you. Any confrontation was bound to lead to a duel because we were not prepared to bow to Welsh intimidation as England teams had done in the past. This was agreed before the game and because of the strength of character that had developed in the side everybody decided to meet fire with fire. Now we were physically prepared to commit ourselves the way the Welsh traditionally did, totally and without consideration for life and limb – either theirs or their opponents'. We had had enough of accepting second-best. This was our last chance, and if we blew it now then there would be nothing left. That was the background to a game of rugby which was buried under more bad publicity than any other, before or since.

By the day of the match, you could cut the atmosphere with a knife. Our supporters kept coming up and saying, 'You've got to win today,' 'You must win,' 'Don't come off the field if you lose.' The Welsh were under exactly the same sort of pressure.

After such a build-up we didn't disappoint the supporters who had come to the bullring. The battle began in the first scrum as both packs smacked into each other. From that point it was just a matter of time before someone was sent off or carried off, or both, which in fact was the case. Even before Paul Ringer was sent off by David Burnett in the fifteenth minute, there were several outbursts and the referee had already issued a general warning. Paul Ringer's late tackle was indicative of the climate and mood of the game, but he had chanced his arm – this time into John Horton's face – once too often. That we applauded the referee and slow hand-clapped Paul Ringer off the field says all you need to know about what we thought of his behaviour. Even before the John Horton late tackle, he had been up to his tricks. Dusty went to collect a high ball and was bowled over by David Richards and Steve Fenwick; the ball went loose and Paul Ringer came charging through to put his knee into the small of Dusty's back. The John Horton affray was not nearly so bad, but Paul Ringer took no notice of his pre-match trial or the referee's general warning and carried on as a law unto himself.

His dismissal did nothing to defuse the situation. From the sending-off position, Dusty put us ahead, but Wales countered immediately when the English scrum lost control near its line and Jeff Squire beat Steve Smith to the touch-down. Well, we had one sent off . . . who was going to be carried off? It turned out to be me! Nearing half-time I went back to gather a rolling ball and, as I gathered, I remembered the golden rule of keeping my back to the opposition to protect the ball and me. Suddenly everything went black as I thought my head was on its way between the posts. I realized that I had received a vicious kick to the head and, as I groggily got to my feet, I could feel the rough edge of flesh where my nose had been split open. There was blood everywhere.

The referee looked a bit horrified and Tony came over to me and said, 'Christ!' Off I went with Don Gatherer to the touchline, where my regular escort, Doctor Leo Walkden, was waiting. Mike Davis came down to the medical room, and after his reaction, I decided to have a look in the mirror at this horror. It wasn't a pretty sight, and now I know what being battle-scarred means. Leo stitched up the wound; the skin was stretched tight and the whole area felt very tender. Mike asked if I wanted to go back. Stupidly, I thought about it for a moment before common sense prevailed and I said no. Mike Rafter came on at half-time to replace me.

Go back to play in that? You must be joking! Scared? Too right. That first forty minutes had knocked the stuffing right out of me. Coming off the field to take a detached view for a few minutes made the whole affair look like a brawl. There was very little rugby in this crazy game; everybody was at each other's throats and growling instead of watching the ball. People were giving 'verbal', being niggly, pushing and generally taking the fun out of rugby. The ball seemed the last concern.

I was interested to see later on television what had necessitated my withdrawal from this cauldron. Very revealing it was, too. No wonder I was shaken. As I had gathered the ball, Geoff Wheel, with a full swing of the boot, had belted my head in a clumsy attempt to hit the ball. If I had faced him, instead of turning my back, there is no knowing what damage he could have done. How much of a face can they sew back on? Whether it was a deliberate action or not, I didn't know, but it certainly was in keeping with what had gone on before. Looking in the mirror, I was worried about the kids. What would they say when they saw their father coming in the next day looking like this? How could I explain that I played rugby because I enjoyed it? As it was, typically, they took no notice at all.

Kris and my folks were watching the game; all this was not very pleasant for them. I felt very disillusioned as I put on my tracksuit and went to sit in the stand. What was the point? Everybody in the stand was agog, watching with their mouths wide open in amazement; like me, they couldn't believe this was happening. The trouble hadn't stopped with my injury. Steve Fenwick completely lost his head and went in with arms and elbows flying; in the end, he also lost Wales the game, though their captain, Jeff Squire, should take some of the blame. I've got a lot of time for Jeff, but you've got to control your side on the field. Instead, there was pandemonium from start to finish.

Dusty's second penalty took us ahead gain, but Wales looked to have sneaked it yet again when Alan Phillips charged down Steve Smith's kick, gathered and fed Elgan Rees, who sped under the posts. Wales, as they had done all afternoon, missed the kick, but they were in front once more. Then, in the dying minute, another Welsh indiscretion allowed Dusty Hare the chance of immortality as he slotted over the winning kick for a 9–8 victory. Rugby, though, was the big loser. Leo Walkden compared the scene in his medical room to the TV series *M.A.S.H.* Candidates for the use of the needles and thread, after me, were Steve Smith, Bill Beaumont, Maurice Colclough, John Scott and Wales's Alan Phillips. Both teams seemed rather stunned that the match had become the blood-bath that everybody had predicted. There was only one thing worse than playing in a game like this, and that was playing in a game like this and losing.

Depressed we may have been but the realization slowly filtered through that we were one game away from the Grand Slam.

It was probably too early to judge the impact of our encounter. And the press, having got what they wanted, made full use of our war zone for material. At the time, I felt like giving the game up; there seemed little point in going on if rugby had degenerated into this. The injury to me was only a part of it; just one incident indicative of the way players were behaving. I was simply unlucky to be in the wrong place at the wrong time.

But a week in sport is a long time, the match was a one-off, and the game against Scotland would offer a chance to make amends. There was a month until that Murrayfield visit and I needed all that time to get myself fit again. The Welsh game was a warning about the dangers of rugby if players forget their duty to the game and to each other. If Twickenham was the agony, then Murrayfield was the ecstasy as English rugby found itself again. Within a few weeks the memory of Twickenham was exorcized by our thrilling attacking display in the first half at Murrayfield.

Prior to the match I was once more able to look round the room at the rest of the lads. I knew we weren't going to blow it, not this time. This England side wasn't about to let go. Reaching this point had been a real team effort. All fifteen, and the bench, had played a full part in making the day possible. From Dusty at full-back right through to Phil Blakeway at prop, everybody knew his job and did it well.

We waited for French referee Monsieur Bonnet's tap on the door. French officials normally allow a flowing game, which was what we wanted, but we had to be careful that this did not lead to our downfall. Over-confidence might allow the Scots to run amok in Murrayfield's wide open spaces. The Scots, with the effervescent Andy Irvine directing operations from full-back, had nothing to lose. What pleasure it would have given them to deny the 'auld enemy' their long-awaited Grand Slam. They'd shown what they were capable of in the game against France. Recovering from a 4–14 deficit, the Scots scored eighteen points in the last thirteen minutes to end their run of thirteen internationals without a win. Andy, who had been in a terrible state in the first half, was the instigator of the revival with two tries and sixteen points – a new record for a Scot. So we had to be on our guard.

Bill took us through our various stretching exercises before we huddled together for his final words of encouragement. 'Come on, now. No mistakes by us, but we've got to punish theirs. Smithy wants good ball, no rubbish. Look, we've got to pull them in on the fringes; if they start standing off, then we drive forward again to make sure they're committed. Right!'

Like a telephone suddenly ringing, the knock on the door grabbed our attention. Referee Bonnet ran his hands over our studs to check they were not dangerous. Eyes met; a mutual look of determination. Just one more time; no mistakes. Seconds later we were running out to a tremendous roar, with Dusty bringing up the rear as usual.

The ground was full. The crowd made even more noise when the blue-shirted warriors took the field. The huddle of white jerseys got together for the national anthem. I defy the Welsh to sing with any more gusto than we did that day. There may be Englishmen who are not as patriotic as the Scots, Welsh or Irish, but none of them were on the Murrayfield pitch as we prepared to give everything for our country.

Suddenly, all the singing and talking was over. It was time for action. My memories of the game are rather vague. The pace of the play was exceptional, even for an international. Yet, rather than wait the whole eighty minutes, we managed to clinch the Grand Slam in the first half hour. By then we had put together three magnificent tries. Whatever the Scots attempted, there was no way we were going to let them get back into the game as the French had done.

The power of our pack made it possible for the backs to cut loose for once. Clive Woodward was the 'hammer of the Scots' – as he would be a year later in the same fixture. Showing a running ability that is rugby's greatest rarity, Clive twice scythed his way through a bemused Scottish defence to make tries for John Carleton and Mike Slemen. Our strong scrum created another try for Carleton when John Scott picked up at number eight. Dusty added the conversion points for the first two scores and our opening surge had taken us sixteen points ahead. The Scots, never ones to take defeat lightly, set about running us off our feet in the second half. Before they got into their stride, there was very nearly a moment of glory for me just after the interval. Steve Smith had set John Scott off near the Scottish line and I was in support to take his return pass. Just for a moment the line seemed within my grasp, but I was brought down by a thundering tackle. Without thinking, I flung back a terrible pass to Steve Smith which could easily have gone anywhere. Luckily, Steve only has to sniff a try. He took the pass above his head to dive over. I was relieved, he was delighted, and England were safe at 23–3.

The Scots stepped up the pace even more. The score quickly became 23–12 before Andy Irvine, always just as likely to lose games as to win them, misjudged a kick by Paul Dodge. John Carleton couldn't have asked for a better bounce as he raced away for the first hat-trick of tries by an English international since 1924. An earlier Dusty penalty meant the score was now 30–12. The Scots had the final word with a superb solo try by fly-half John Rutherford. Irvine's conversion made it 30–18, but we had done it! My initial reaction at the final whistle was relief – I had pulled a rib cartilage whilst attempting to tackle Keith Robertson midway through the second half. With Tony Neary also suffering from a badly bruised calf, the English back row had just about run out of steam. In my case the pain was bad and, after a brief encounter with Don Gatherer on the touchline, I had been in two minds about whether to go off. But Bill pressed me to stick it out. After all, I had left the field in England's previous two internationals – three in a row would have been an unenviable record. So I stayed on, although I'm not sure how effective I was in those dying minutes.

When the final whistle went, we all bolted for the changing rooms. In the tunnel the Scots looked disappointed; but they shouldn't have done. There was no disgrace in a defeat like this. Our faces were dominated by huge grins as we beamed 'Well done' and 'Congratulations' to one another.

A great day. A great season.

Notes on the Contributors

MARK BAILEY played rugby for Cambridge University, Wasps, Barbarians and England, for whom he won seven caps between 1984 and 1990. He has now returned to Cambridge as a Fellow and Admissions Tutor at Gonville and Caius College and Lecturer in Local History at the university. He has published numerous books and articles on medieval English society, including on the importance of the rabbit to the medieval English economy, which was the topic of his doctoral thesis. He has also found time to write occasional articles on rugby. Since 1993 he has represented the university on the RFU committee.

SIMON BARNES has for some years been the acclaimed general sporting columnist for *The Times*. He has published several books, including a biography of the cricketer Phil Edmonds and two on wildlife. He played junior rugby for Emmanuel School – though by his own admission he preferred to slope off to the pub if he could. Since then he has played soccer, including four years as a goal-keeper for a team of foreign devils in Hong Kong, where he lived for four years.

STUART BARNES enjoyed a long and distinguished rugby-playing career with Bath RFC, where he made a great contribution to the extraordinary run of success of the club. While he was there the club won no fewer than eight Pilkington Cups and five league championships; he was the club captain when they won the cup and league double for the first time. During that time he also won ten caps for England at fly-half. He retired early, and is now a rugby presenter for Sky TV, a columnist on the *Daily Telegraph* and author of a successful autobiography, *Smelling of Roses* – which, unusually among sporting autobiographies, he actually wrote himself.

JON CALLARD played for Newport for five years before moving to Bath in 1989. He has played there ever since. He received his first cap for England in 1993, played for Barbarians in 1995 and was a member of the 1995 World Cup squad in South Africa.

RAY GRAVELL enjoyed a distinguished rugby-playing career: he played for Llanelli from 1969 to 1985, and was club captain from 1980 to 1982. He won numerous caps for Wales between 1975 and 1982, and went on one tour with the British Lions. He also played for Barbarians and Irish Wolfhounds. Since retirement he has established himself in a dual career as a broadcaster with BBC Wales and as an actor, taking leading roles in numerous TV series and cinema films.

DAVID GREEN was born in 1939 and educated at Oxford, where he was a cricket blue in 1959, 1960 and 1961. He played cricket professionally with Lancashire from 1959 to 1967 and for Gloucestershire from 1968 until his retirement in 1971, achieving the honour of being one of *Wisden*'s Five Cricketers of the Year in 1969. Meanwhile he played club rugby at a high level, first for Sale (1958–67), starting as a centre but spending most of that period in the back row. When cricket took him south the Bristol club recruited him to captain the 2nd XV, which he did from 1968 to 1971, then becoming coach and finally a selector. He has worked as a cricket correspondent on the *Daily Telegraph* since 1982.

DAVID HANDS was born in 1947 and brought up in Salisbury. There he played for the local club's 3rd XV and attended Bishop Wordsworth's Grammar School, playing for the school 2nd XV. He later read history at Fitzwilliam College, Cambridge, playing for the college 2nd XV. He began his career as a journalist on the

184

newsdesk of the *South Wales Argus*, later moving on to the *Leicester Mercury* and eventually *The Times*. There, he succeeded Peter West as rugby correspondent in 1983, and has remained in that post ever since, covering eight overseas tours and all three World Cups to date.

TIM HEALD played rugby at school at Sherborne, and has remained keenly interested in it, along with most other sports. As a writer he is an all-rounder, having published many crime novels and a variety of non-fiction, including biographies of such wildly differing characters as Prince Philip, Barbara Cartland, Brian Johnston and Denis Compton. He has also written widely on sport, especially cricket, and is currently completing a book on the last years of Hong Kong as a British colony.

DAMIAN HOPLEY was born in London in 1970, and plays rugby for Wasps, Barbarians and England. He was a member of the England squad in South Africa for the third World Cup, in which he played as a replacement against Western Samoa. He also won a Cambridge blue in 1992, and was a member of the England side that won the World Cup Sevens in 1993. As a student at St Andrews he read theology, emerging with the degree of Master of Theology; but at least for the moment he has signed up for Mammon, working for a firm of city brokers. In his spare time he is a keen blues pianist, and on the 1995 World Cup tour he was judge of the players' court.

STEPHEN JONES played rugby for the lower XVs at Newport and London Welsh. He has been rugby correspondent of the *Sunday Times* for over ten years, throughout which time he also edited *Rothmans Rugby Union Yearbook*. He has also published several books on rugby union, one of which, *Endless Winter*, won the William Hill prize for best sports book of 1993.

FRANK KEATING has won a wide following for his regular sports column in the *Guardian*. He has won eight senior Fleet Street awards for his work, which has included articles for *Punch* and for the *Spectator*. He also writes a column for *Rugby World*. After thirty years of wandering the sports stadia and arenas of the world, he has recently returned to Herefordshire, where he was born, and where he now lives with his wife and two children.

ALLAN MASSIE was educated at Glenalmond and Trinity College, Cambridge. He was a sports columnist for several years with the *Glasgow Herald*, and has written on rugby for the *Scotsman* and the Scottish *Daily Mail*. He is a prolific novelist and journalist. Among his books is *A Portrait of Scottish Rugby* (1984). He lives in the Scottish Borders and is a keen member of Selkirk RFC.

MIKE SEABROOK has had a keen interest in rugby since his schooldays. Although born with a body that refuses obstinately to do what he tells it, so that he could never play the game, he enjoyed trying for various more or less coarse rugby sides; and he derived vast enjoyment from the beer and the rude songs on the coach afterwards. He has worked as a police officer, adman and computer pundit. Since dropping out of everything in 1989 to become a full-time author, he has written four novels, an insider's view of the workings of the police and biographies of the composers Peter Maxwell Davies and Richard Rodney Bennett, and edited several anthologies of new writing on sport. He is currently working on a biography of the linguist, philosopher and political dissident, Noam Chomsky.

TIAN STRAUSS plays rugby at number eight for Western Province of South Africa. There he has also won eleven caps for the international side, for which he has scored three tries so far, including one against England in 1992. He is a trainee lawyer by profession, currently in articles and taking his law examinations.

ROGER UTTLEY played for England twenty-three times as lock, number eight or flanker between 1973 and 1981, being captain in 1977 and an ever-present in Bill Beaumont's Grand Slam side. He spent most of his playing career with the Gosforth club, with a couple of seasons at Wasps. Since his retirement from playing he has written three books on rugby: an autobiography, *Pride in England*, a coaching manual and, with David Frost, a book on captaincy. He has also gained himself an OBE for services to sport and an MA in leisure and recreational activities. He is now Director of Physical Education at Harrow School.